# ISSUES IN ACQUISITIONS

## LIBRARY MANAGEMENT SERIES

Number one: Planning-Programming-Budgeting System: Implications for Library Management

Number two: Legal Reference Collections for Non-Law Libraries: A Survey of Holdings in the Academic Community

Number three: Library Budgeting: Critical Challenges for the Future

Number four: Emerging Trends in Library Organization: What Influences Change

Number five: Serials Collection Development: Choices and Strategies

Number six: Reference Service: A Perspective

Number seven: Library Fundraising: Vital Margin for Excellence

Number eight: Issues in Acquisitions: Programs & Evaluation

# ISSUES IN ACQUISITIONS:
## PROGRAMS & EVALUATION

edited by
Sul H. Lee
Dean, University Libraries
Professor of Bibliography
The University of Oklahoma

THE PIERIAN PRESS
1984

Library of Congress Catalog Card Number 84-61226
ISBN 0-87650-188-9



THE PIERIAN PRESS
P.O. Box 1808
Ann Arbor, MI. 48106

For Melissa

# Contents

Introduction . . . . . . . . . . . . . . . . . . . . . . . . . . . . . . . . . . . . . ix

The Preparation of Guidelines for Evaluating Performance of Vendors for In-Print Monographs . . . . . . . . . . . . . . 1
*Noreen S. Alldredge*

Evaluating Approval Plan Vendor Performance: Toward a Rationale and Model . . . . . . . . . . . . . . . . . . . 11
*Gary M. Shirk*

Evaluating the Role and Effectiveness of Approval Plans for Library Collection Development . . . . . . . . . . . 33
*Stanley P. Hodge*

Librarian-Faculty Role in Collection Development with Approval Programs . . . . . . . . . . . . . . . . . . . . . . . . 55
*Sara Ramser Beck*

Evaluating and Selecting an Automated Acquisition System . . . 69
*Edna Laughrey* and *Mary Kay Murray*

Coping with Library Needs: The Approval Vendor's Response/Responsibility . . . . . . . . . . . . . . . . . . . . . . . 91
*Dana L. Alessi*

The Approval Plan – The Core of an Academic Wholesaler's Business . . . . . . . . . . . . . . . . . . . . . . . . 111
*Gloria Frye* and *Marcia Romanansky*

Bibliography . . . . . . . . . . . . . . . . . . . . . . . . . . . . . . . . . . . . . 121
*Rodney M. Hersberger*

Index . . . . . . . . . . . . . . . . . . . . . . . . . . . . . . . . . . . . . . . . . 131

# Introduction

On March 19 and 20, 1984, a conference in Oklahoma City examined current issues in library acquisitions. The conference – Issues in Acquisitions: Programs and Evaluation attracted seventy-five librarians from Canada and the U.S. Topics covered included guidelines for evaluating vendor performance, evaluating approval plans performance, the effectiveness of approval plans for collection development, faculty-librarian interface in collection development and approval plans, automated acquisitions systems, and approval programs from the vendor's perspective.

Library acquisitions, their costs, and procedures used to acquire library materials are constantly debated issues. This volume is intended to convey the sense of the speaker's presentations through publication of their papers. There are both practical and theoretical approaches to the current issues in library acquisitions. It was clear from the papers that approval plans play a major role in academic library collection development. It was also agreed that both the library and the vendor have major, defined responsibilities to make an approval plan a successful collection development tool. In fact, it was assumed that the library and the vendor have a partnership to ensure a successful approval program. Many libraries are also actively planning to automate their acquisitions functions to enhance processing and efficiency.

Seven formal papers were presented at the conference, each being followed by a period of questions to the speakers and discussion among the participants. Unfortunately, the often provocative discussions cannot be reported here. The speakers and their papers were 1) Noreen S. Alldredge (Dean of Libraries, Montana State University), "Preparation of Guidelines for Evaluation of Vendor Performance"; 2) Gary M. Shirk (Head of Acquisitions, University of Minnesota), "Evaluating Approval Plan Vendor Performance"; 3) Stanley P. Hodge (Head of Resource Development Division, Texas A&M University), "Evaluating the Role and Effectiveness of Approval Plans for Library Collection Development"; 4) Sara Ramser Beck

(Acquisitions Librarian, Washington University), ("Librarian-Faculty Role in Collection Development in Libraries with Approval Programs") 5) Edna Laughrey (Head of Acquisitions and Book Fund Accounting, University of Michigan), "Evaluating and Selecting an Automated Acquisitions System"; 6) Dana Alessi (Division Sales Manager, Blackwell North America, Inc.), "Coping with Library Needs: The Approval Vendor's Response/Responsibility"; 7) Gloria Frye (Manager, Technical Sales, Baker & Taylor Company), "The Approval Program – The Core of an Academic Wholesaler's Business."

The University of Oklahoma Foundation, Inc. was a conference cosponsor with the University of Oklahoma Libraries. The Foundation's Executive Director, Ron D. Burton, was very supportive of this program and warmly welcomed our conference participants.

Three other people contributed to the Conference and this volume. Rodney Hersberger was Conference Coordinator, prepared the Bibliography and Index, and provided editorial assistance in preparing this volume. Pat Webb also provided excellent overall administrative support to the Conference and this book's preparation. Coy Harmon also offered superb editorial assistance.

Sul H. Lee
Norman, Oklahoma
March 27, 1984

# THE PREPARATION OF GUIDELINES FOR EVALUATING PERFORMANCE OF VENDORS FOR IN-PRINT MONOGRAPHS

by

Noreen S. Alldredge

*Introduction*

At the 1981 Midwinter Conference of the American Library Association, the Collection Management and Development Committee appointed a subcommittee to formulate guidelines for evaluating the performance of vendors. As the subcommittee began to address the task, it soon became evident that we were charting fairly unexplored waters and that some narrowing of the vendor category would be necessary. Today our valiant group is preparing the sixth draft for review at the 1984 Annual Conference of ALA, and we hope the guidelines will be published in late 1984 or shortly thereafter.

The subcommittee members are: Tom Leonhardt, University of Oregon; Linda Pletzke, Library of Congress; Marion Reid, Louisiana State University; and myself. We have been greatly assisted by many people who have reviewed the drafts. Those who have made significant contributions are: Caroline Early, George Washington University; Sara Heitshu, University of Michigan; and Gay Henderson, Ohio State University.

Our meetings at ALA Conferences have been eventful because great forces of nature, like snowstorms and conflicts in ALA meeting schedules, kept all four members of the subcommittee from even being in the same place at the same time until a couple of months ago. Nevertheless, phone calls and drafts via the postal system did get us started.

There have been many times when I personally wanted to donate the total project to the "recycle bin," especially when I felt no progress was being made. Yet, I look back and see that the current draft is taking shape and that it is an improvement over our first efforts. We are hopeful that a decade from now the guidelines will have evolved into useful standards.

I do not intend to present the drafted guidelines nor to give all the points of the study, but I would like to review the whats, whys, and hows for evaluating the performance of vendors and to discuss where we go from here.

*What Do We Mean By Vendor Performance Guidelines?*

A study at Louisiana State University by Sandra Stokley and Marion Reid which was published in 1978 gives one the best justifications for assessing vendor performance. "In a time of rising costs and reduced budgets, the acquisitions departments in libraries must determine which book dealers are serving them most. Positive and negative aspects of the dealers' services can be weighed thus enabling personnel to decide which dealers to use in particular situations. No rigid rules can be established. Instead, guidelines can be formed for the purposes of ordering, hopefully resulting in services that meet the needs of a particular library." (Stokley and Reid, 1978)

G. Edward Evans (1979) in his book *Developing Library Collections* summarizes the basic factor in establishing a working relationship between libraries and jobbers:

What libraries expect from jobbers:
1) large inventory of titles
2) prompt and accurate order fulfillment
3) prompt and accurate reporting on items not in stock
4) personal service at a reasonable price

What jobbers expect of libraries:
1) time to get to know what the library needs
2) cooperation in placing orders
3) keeping paperwork to a minimum
4) prompt payment for services

These expectations carry responsibilities on both sides. For the librarian's part it seems that some checks on the vendor's abilities would be necessary before entering into a working relationship, and at the same time it would be necessary to ensure that internal library procedures were as efficient as possible. At this stage, it would behoove the librarian to reaffirm why a vendor is being used – namely, service. And it would be useful to think of why the vendor performs the service – namely, profit. If each keeps the other's motivating force in mind, there will be much less chance of misunderstanding.

Conducting an assessment of vendor performance will identify and yield quantitative and qualitative data on how well a vendor meets the needs of a specific library.

The guidelines as currently drafted deliberately avoid the position of giving expert opinion yet it is hoped that standards will evolve. In the meantime, there will be a gap between guidelines and a national standard, or even regional standards, until more studies have been completed. The present guidelines walk a tightrope between methodological precision and the feasibility of an actual study.

I said earlier that I was not going to reproduce the proposed guidelines nor even go through the major points of a study. However, let me note here that Stokley and Reid (1978) identified the ideal way to conduct a study, namely, "to order the same title from each dealer on the same day in volume. However, in times of reduced budgets, this is not practical. Indeed, not many libraries would want five copies of many books." This type of study was done in 1973 at Indiana State University and was published in *LRTS* (Kim 1975). Whether you would conduct an "ideal" study or not should not prohibit you from an occasional investigation of just how well your acquisition needs are being met. Tantamount to most of our acquisition efforts are three primary areas open to assessment:

1) quality of service

2) turnaround/receipt time

3) discount

Areas 2 and 3 can be more easily assessed and lend themselves to statistical study. Turnaround/receipt times are easily measured, though discounts can be more difficult because of the frequent changes in pricing policies. Area 1, the quality of service, is very individualized, yet it should be detailed in discussions with a vendor or assessment cannot be made if expectations are not defined. Each library will have varying factors to consider. For example, what trade-offs are important? Does geography make a difference in time and service?

We must have statistically valid ways to monitor the service (or discount or turnaround/receipt time) which a vendor provides. This need has led to the creation of the guidelines. One of our greatest challenges has been to prepare a section on the statistical validity of studies which may be conducted. We are confident that the next draft addresses this challenge in a meaningful way. In addition to the statistical aspect, we have prepared a section which is addressed to automated systems.

*Why Do We Need to Assess Vendor Performance?*

Several years ago I was fortunate to be in the audience when Ralph Nader spoke to some university students. One of the things he advised them to do when interviewing for jobs was to ask the prospective employer if they could bring their conscience to work. It seems to me we should each do that and when we do, we have some responsibilities to uphold.

I am always considerably irritated by librarians who cannot appreciate that while many of us may work in what are considered non-profit institutions, there is no group with a profit and loss ledger like a library's. Every time a client leaves without getting some portion of what s/he wanted, we have lost a future customer or worse yet we will have an enemy in the legislature. Now I am not suggesting that we can or should have everything our clients want, but we can assist, refer and redirect. In other words, we need to deserve as well as want their repeat business.

We have kept ourselves in the power position of disseminating information to only some clients for too long. And we have believed ourselves removed from the business world for too long also. It is time to take off the white gloves and apply some basic principles of sound management.

What do we buy and from whom? What services, discounts, speed factors are at work in the acquisition process? If we can see ourselves as businesses with profit and loss dimensions, then we need to assess our performance and that of the vendors we utilize. Most of us order from jobbers (vendors) rather than direct from the publisher, although at least one study has been done which indicated ordering from the publisher was best for that particular library. Due to the subject matter of the needed materials in a library, a large portion of what we acquire is general trade books and so we tend to use vendors.

Consequently, there is a need to assess these vendors in an objective, consistent and frequent manner. There is much to be gained for librarians and vendors from a review of the order process starting with a library's formulation of the request until receipt of the title. Improvement in procedures and fulfillment are probably needed at several steps in the process, beginning in our own acquisitions departments. It would help if we took a good look at our internal operations and then moved on to review the vendor's performance.

While I am on my soapbox, let me share with you a principle which I find essential to management. If something goes wrong, examine your own role first. For example, did you not make clear what you wanted done? Did you fail to provide direction or a realistic time frame? I am sure you get the idea. If you are confident of the clarity and efficiency of your procedures, then by all means make a thorough examination of the performance of your vendor(s).

Many libraries select vendors based on subjective impressions of the staff, and while staff can frequently provide valid input to the final selection of a vendor, librarians would do well to conduct a study of performance based on an analysis of actual order/receipt success and failure. A statistical analysis of discount and fulfillment may be negated by problems in quality of service. So a combination of objective and subjective reviews is needed.

The reality of the supply/demand situation is as Robert Lincoln (1978) noted a few years ago: "Open discussion of trade efficiency is one way to improve service and contribute to knowledge about the trade. Publishers and distributors know their current stock but do not have the time to analyze their supply patterns, except in specific instances. Accordingly, it is up to librarians to take the initiative and circulate the results of their activities; with enough feedback both service and knowledge will benefit."

The acquisitions world does have a folklore. We can all cite horror cases of orders gone astray, wrong titles sent, reports of a title being reported out of print and then we find we can get it if we go directly to the publisher. Errors are what we are more likely to recall. Like all folklore, time serves to embellish the story and so it is a foolish librarian who selects vendors on the basis of casual information instead of facts. Certainly some of the folklore began with facts, and many of the horror stories could be repeated today. Many of us believe a vendor will report hard-to-get titles as out of print because these are more expensive to acquire. Almost twenty years ago, Daniel Melcher (1966) noted in an *LJ* article, "I have long had a rather strong suspicion that some jobbers were not above using this method to avoid making delivery of books on which they could not get maximum discounts."

A comparison of American in-print vendors done at the University of Utah and reported by Margaret Landesman and Christopher Gates (1980) in *Library Acquisitions* drew this conclusion: "Given the extent to which the study differed from our preconceptions, and variations in vendor performance over time, access to similar studies on a regular basis would be very useful."

We need to conduct studies to determine the facts. We need to conduct studies to ascertain wherein lies the responsibility for problems. I once worked on a campus where postal service deliveries were made to the library twice a day. We could not understand why the titles from our major vendor took so long to reach us in comparison to several smaller vendors with whom we also did business. We finally discovered that trucking lines had to deliver to a central service point and then campus labor and trucks brought boxes to the library. Campus service would wait until they had a "van load" and this, of course, resulted in considerable delays until we discovered what was happening and got them to agree to bring us whatever they had each day. The "van load" system added a significant delay in receipt of titles and would have unfairly skewed any vendor study under way at the time. As it was, we almost condemned the vendor before we examined all our own procedures. So the successful acquisition of materials will benefit from a thorough examination in and out of house.

*What Is the Role of the Professional Association and What Has Been Done to Date?*

Our interest in securing the best deal is based on a need to acquire materials promptly. Yet these days of limited financial resources as well as significant inflation rates sometimes change our definition of the best deal.

Libraries and librarians have not, generally speaking, been cost conscious in the past. Now, however, since we are more aware of the need to maximize resource dollars, and if you will take up my plea that we need to be aware of the profit/loss aspects of our business, we are indeed anxious to get the most for each dollar. In addition, automation has enabled us to examine our procedures and expectations by providing us with management information not readily available before.

You may wonder if a national professional association should take a role in the preparation of guidelines. But these guidelines follow others which the Bookdealer Library Relations and the Collection Management and Development Committees of the Resources and Technical Services Divisions of ALA have previously issued, and those were welcomed by librarians. Fifteen years ago RTSD/ALA published a study titled *Purchasing Library Materials in Public and School Libraries*, which was prepared by Evelyn Hensel and Peter Veillette for ALA and the National League of Cities. It is a handy book which contains a set of guiding principles for determining the qualifications of wholesalers. It does note that quantitative standards may be developed later but cautions that "it would not be possible to draw up any simple quantitative standards because of the many variables that would have to be taken into account . . . ." (Hensel and Veillette, 1969)

The Bookdealer Library Relations Committee issued acquisitions guidelines in the 1970s for in-print monographs, serials and periodicals and microforms. These were intended to guide the librarian in placing orders accurately and providing publishers with the information necessary to fulfill orders accurately.

ALA also published in 1973 a basic work entitled *The Acquisition of Library Materials* as the result of a recommendation from RTSD and the Library Education Division that there was a need for a handbook that could be used in all libraries, regardless of size.

While all these efforts were of great use in the preparation of orders, they did not usually address the methods by which librarians could assess performance. One publication which called for this was *Melcher on Acquisition*. In this 1971 ALA monograph, Daniel Melcher in discussing how long it should take to obtain a book, wrote "One step in the right direction would be to monitor performance and really let top management know how things are." (Melcher 1971)

Prior to the 1970s, library literature has only a few articles related to vendor performance. Most of those are subjective assessments or are focused on approval plan performance. The vendor's point of view is also scarce in the literature. What little there is reflects a suspicion as to what libraries and librarians will do with the results of studies. There is a humorous suggestion that rankings might not be unlike Olympic competition, as well as a more serious request to share results of studies with dealers.

Some libraries became interested in vendor performance after a major vendor went bankrupt and libraries were left with hundreds of outstanding orders. However, institutions who had been monitoring performance, by spot checks or careful study, were forewarned and able to transfer all business or at least spread some of it out ahead of the default.

That experience combined with the trend of the 1970s to assess everything from Vietnam to our quality of life, to the responsibility of corporate society, to what was happening at work led to evaluation in all arenas of the library world. We are still in that evaluative era – we analyze our collection strengths, we assess our job performance, we write goals and objectives, not to mention mission statements, and we have even begun to come to grips with the reality that much of what we have bought has never been used. Naturally, this has made the acquisition process eligible for a thorough scrutiny also.

As library schools have focused on new directions in curriculum or have not addressed the applied techniques needed, librarians have looked to their professional associations for continuing education, seminars and workshops, and publications which can meet their needs. With all the acquisition related information which is out there, the librarian beginning acquisition work as well as those who are taking time to conduct evaluations of service have felt a need to conduct statistically valid studies of vendor performance; hence, the drafts currently underway to offer guidelines.

### *Ethics of Studies and Where Do We Go from Here?*

As we become more attentive consumer advocates, we must address the ethical issues present in assessing performance. Different opinions are held about to whom results of vendor studies should be disseminated and whether dealers should be named. There is agreement that the vendors should know the results regarding their services and these results should be the basis for discussion of services and expectations. Whether the dealers to which one vendor is compared should be identified to other vendors or to colleagues is still being debated.

Some vendors welcome full disclosure. If a decision is made to identify dealers and disseminate information through publication, then full details of how the information was gathered and all factors which may affect the results should be included. Vendors involved should be given the opportunity to respond to the findings before publication of the results so that any pertinent factors unknown to the librarian can be included. Vendors may wish to develop a rating system for acquisition departments. Turn-about is fair play.

Caution should be taken before locally applying the results of a vendor study from another institution. Factors affecting one library's study may not be relevant in another. Decisions regarding dealer selection should never be based solely on a vendor study done in another library. However, results of several studies compared with one's own can give a broader base on which to confirm or question one's conclusions. Each library must in the final analysis assign priorities to vendor services and select the vendor which meets those priorities – be they discount, speed, accuracy, etc. Generally, no one supplier will be best for everything.

A finished study reflects past performance and can be used for tomorrow's orders. We should continue to build upon the base of cooperation and interdependence which exists between library and vendor. Increased communication, even if it's to resolve problems (be they perceived or real) can only help. In reporting the BOS (Book Order System) developed at the University of Massachusetts, Amherst, Janet Uden wrote: "The BOS vendor performance report is a very useful tool in helping to evaluate our jobbers. It is a tool that has been discussed with our major vendors so that when we critique their performance with them they understand how the information was gathered. We have found through these discussions that mutual trust is built and, in the long run, is beneficial to both parties." (Uden 1980)

The basis of the relationship of library and vendor was clearly defined in the Bookdealer Library Relations publication *Guidelines for Handling Library Orders for In-Print Monographic Publications*: "Librarians and bookdealers conduct their business on a contractual basis, whether formal or informal. Librarians should realize that their own contribution to efficiency is of paramount importance. Responsibilities, routines and procedures within the library must be under continuous scrutiny to ensure that they achieve the best results. All successful relationships depend on the goodwill and cooperation of both parties. Continuing discussion of goals, needs and problems is an integral part of every relationship between librarian and bookdealer." (Bookdealer Library Relations Committee, 1972)

Information is the basis of life for libraries and library users. Is it not time we gathered more information about the actual process of acquiring information?

## References


American Library Association, Bookdealer Library Relations Committee. 1972. *Guidelines for Handling Library Orders for In-Print Monographic Publications*. Chicago: American Library Association.

American Library Association, Bookdealer Library Relations Committee. 1974. *Guidelines for Handling Library Orders for Serials and Periodicals*. Chicago: American Library Association.

American Library Association, Bookdealer Library Relations Committee. 1977. *Guidelines for Handling Library Orders for Microforms*. Chicago: American Library Association.

Berkner, Dimity S. 1979. "Communication Between Vendors and Librarians: The Bookseller's Point of View." *Library Acquisitions: Practice & Theory* 3:85--90.

Bullard, Scott R. 1979. "Where's Ralph Nader Now That Acquisitions Librarians Need Him?" *Library Acquisitions: Practice & Theory* 3:1--2.

Evans, G. Edward. 1979. "Distributors of Library Materials." *Developing Library Collections*. Littleton, CO: Libraries Unlimited.

Ford, Stephen. 1973. *The Acquisition of Library Materials*. Chicago: American Library Association.

Kim, Ung Chon. 1975. "Purchasing Books from Publishers and Wholesalers." *Library Resources and Technical Services*. 19: 133–47.

Landesman, Margaret and Christopher Gates. 1980. "Performance of American In-Print Vendors: A Comparison at the University of Utah." *Library Acquisitions: Practice & Theory* 4:187--92

Lincoln, Robert. 1978. "Vendors and Delivery: An Analysis of Selected Publishers, Publisher/Agents, Distributors, and Wholesalers." *Canadian Library Journal* 35:51–55,57.

Melcher, Daniel. 1966. "When Is a Book Really O/P?" *Library Journal* 91:4576--8.

Melcher, Daniel. 1971. *Melcher on Acquisition*. Chicago: American Library Association.

Stokley, Sandra L. and Marion T. Reid. 1978. "A Study of Five Book Dealers Used by Louisiana State University Library." *Library Resources and Technical Services* 22:117–25.

Uden, Janet. 1980. "Financial Reporting and Vendor Performance: A Case Study." *Journal of Library Automation* vol. 13, no. 3: 185–95 (September 1980).

Veenstra, John and Lois Mai. 1962. "When Do You Use a Jobber?" *College and Research Libraries* 23:522--4.

# EVALUATING APPROVAL PLAN VENDOR PERFORMANCE: TOWARD A RATIONALE AND MODEL

by

Gary M. Shirk

## *Introduction*

Despite two decades of approval plan use, a great deal of critical attention in the literature, and four international conferences, approval plan vendor performance evaluation remains relatively unexplored. Articles such as those by Gregor and Fraser,[1] Hulbert and Curry,[2] and Leonhardt[3] provide useful examples of vendor appraisals, but, like all case histories, their usefulness is limited to libraries with similar circumstances. Broader applicability would require a performance evaluation model built upon a general rationale whose characteristics were not limited to those feasible in a single library situation. The model's elements could then be shaped to respond to individual variations among libraries while providing vendors with assurances of fair and equitable appraisal.

This paper responds to the need for such a model. Released from the practical limitations of a particular set of library circumstances, it develops a general rationale by exploring the nature of key library/ vendor relationships and their implications for vendor performance evaluation. It then derives design specifications from these observations and describes a vendor performance evaluation model which satisfies them.

## *Rationale*

At the present time, there is no well defined approach to studies of book dealer performance. The ALA RTSD Resources Section's Collection Management and Development Committee is currently working on the sixth draft of its "Guidelines for Evaluating Performance of Vendors for In-Print Monographs" scheduled for release late summer or fall, 1984.[4] Although portions of these guidelines may be applicable to approval plan vendor evaluation, they do not obviate the need to develop appraisal techniques that recognize the special library/vendor relationships which approval plans create. The nature of these relationships may have profound implications for the way in which we evaluate vendor performance. This section, therefore, describes significant library/vendor relationships and explains their implications for designing an approval plan vendor evaluation.

*1. Approval plan vendors primarily provide services, not commodities.*

Citing a colleague, Wolf observes that the vendor is the library's representative, not a source of supply.[5] This rather commonplace observation is, nevertheless, profound in its impact on the appraisal of vendors, particularly approval vendors.

A source of supply provides a commodity. If that commodity is easily replicated or essentially undifferentiated (e.g., winter wheat), various sources of supply can provide the "same" product. If the commodity is difficult to replicate or unique (e.g., book titles), the source of supply can be restricted by the producer of the commodity. For example, publishers who do not sell to vendors restrict the source of supply to themselves.

In contrast, service providers are not so closely linked to the producer of a commodity. The focus of their activity is not the commodity they provide but the value they add to that commodity by virtue of their services. Although approval plan vendors have characteristics of both suppliers and service providers, their real value to libraries rests in the services they provide. Their continued existence, therefore, depends upon the variety of these services and the level of performance they can achieve in them.

However, offering services is not enough; vendors must compete with others to provide those services:

a. They both cooperate and compete with publishers to distribute materials to libraries;

b. They compete with other book dealers who provide similar services; and

c. They compete with libraries who frequently believe they can provide the same or better service for themselves at a lower cost.

Recognizing this competitive milieu, libraries evaluating vendors should focus on their services and the value that those services add to the materials that they receive. Libraries should recognize the full range of the vendor's services and extend their appraisal broadly, rather than focus on any single service when conducting their evaluation.

*2. Each library is unique.*

Libraries operating approval plans are socio-political organizations that differ from each other as much as one person differs from another. There are good reasons for these differences. Operational policies and procedures will be as different as the local traditions from which they emerge. In one library context, faculty may have a key role in evaluating approval materials; in another, faculty may have no role at all. For one institution broad coverage is essential, and the library will depend upon the vendor to gather materials from the universe of publishers over the full range of subjects. Another library will seek delivery speed and be willing to forego discount to achieve it. As McCullough cautions, "one library's experience cannot be transferred directly to another without allowances for the specific library setting."[6]

The implications for libraries evaluating approval vendors are clear. Reported evaluations of approval vendor performance at other institutions provide, at best, general indications of performance and methodological guidelines. There is no substitute for local, library specific analysis of vendor performance. The library must evaluate the plan in its own setting, explicitly stating and weighting the performance criteria which it feels is most important.

*3. The approval plan vendor/library relationship is a contract.*

American legal tradition describes a contract as an agreement between two or more parties for the exchange of what the parties consider equivalents.[7] The nature of the agreement is constrained only by statute or legal rules that may affect it in whole or in part.[8] Although vendor/library approval plan agreements vary in their formality from institution to institution,[9] it is clear that a state of contract exists when library and vendor establish a relationship that is purposeful, voluntary and created for their mutual benefit. The vendor agrees to provide a range of services, including the provision of library materials to be selected or rejected by the library in accordance with a pre-established profile. The library in return agrees to fulfill a number of responsibilities in which prompt payment of invoices is paramount.

Mosher and Biblarz have used courtship and marriage as analogies to characterize the creation of an approval plan agreement. During courtship, dealers are likely to exaggerate their charms,[10] while moonstruck libraries blind themselves to potential flaws that may later endanger the plan's success. Once the agreement has been reached, the library and vendor are bound to each other in a relationship that may last for many years. Separation of course is possible, but, like divorce, can be painful and costly for both.[11] The vendor, who loses an approval client, may lose both sales volume and customer credibility. The library, on the other hand, risks delayed or missed books, forced changes to procedures, and possible staffing reassignments. Furthermore, if the library changes to another vendor, it will be required to accommodate the new vendor's procedures and forms, the increased costs of managerial oversight, and the added returns during the early months of the new plan.[12]

If the approval plan agreement is an implicit contract between the library and vendor, it can be a useful vehicle for clarifying mutual expectations, responsibilities, and benefits. To be an effective participant in negotiation of the agreement, the library should know in advance of the agreement it needs, the performance required of the plan to satisfy those needs, and the level of performance it must require of itself to satisfy the terms of the agreement. In view of the potential disruption to both parties, the terms and conditions for separation should minimize the risk to both the library and the vendor. It should specify under what performance conditions would either the library or the vendor terminate the plan, how would the decision to terminate be implemented and in what time frame.

4. *The approval plan relationship is intense, extremely complicated and of long duration. Its success depends upon consistent communication.*

All major vendors supplying domestic approval plan services ship weekly,[13] and, depending upon the reliability of the shipping services, libraries unpack, evaluate and promptly authorize payments for the materials received each week. Depending upon the size of the plan, the flow of material can be an intermittent trickle or an unrelenting deluge, both without predetermined end. In either case, however, its course has been determined by the subject and non-subject parameters of the profile and how they are mutually understood by both the people who supply the materials and those in the library who accept or reject them.

The more people involved and the more fragmented and differentiated the profile, the more complicated and difficult the task. It's often difficult to get two people to understand even simple matters in the same way. Attempting to merge the understanding of a group of 10, 20, 30 or even more people whose membership may be constantly changing is a task that borders on the impossible. Recognizing this difficulty, well designed approval plans acknowledge the importance of communication[14] and formalize procedures to assure frequent contacts with their approval vendors.[15,16]

The importance of communications at each phase of the plan's life is well recognized in the literature. Pickett urges that the library staff responsible for vendor selection seek the early involvement of anyone who will be selecting materials supplied through the plan.[17] Articles by Evans and Argyres[18] and Gregor and Fraser[19] point out that written profiling tools improve communication and increase the likelihood of the plan's success. Others note the importance of exchanging information about library and vendor processing,[20,21] an exchange that Cargill observes has been improved by the practice of hiring librarians as vendor sales representatives.[22] Gregor and Fraser also emphasize that communications is a joint responsibility shared by the vendor and the library.[23]

A vendor performance evaluation process should, therefore, include provisions for systematic library/vendor communications. If communication is a joint responsibility, then both library and vendor may be expected to initiate inquiries and receive prompt responses. The need for communication begins during the selection process and extends throughout the relationship; it is fundamental both to the success of the plan and to the vendor's ability to perform as expected.

5. *The library and the vendor co-produce observed approval plan performance.*

The observed results of frequently cited approval plan performance measures, such as discount, speed of title arrival, overdue titles claimed, rejection rates, etc. are often as much due to actions attributable to libraries as they are due to vendor performance. However, the complexity of approval plan operations often obscures the library's role. The relationship is analogous to the way in which markets are described as the simultaneous operation of two functions: supply and demand. The market (observed quantity of goods sold) is due to *both* supply and demand rather than to either separately. Without demand, there would be no sales, regardless of supply; without supply, demand alone can't create sales. On the one hand, we are attempting to sell coal in Newcastle; on the other, we are lining up to buy tickets for a passenger flight to Mars. There's no market in either case. Likewise, observed vendor performance can be described as the simultaneous operation of two functions: library behavior and vendor behavior.

The clearest illustration of this observation is perhaps the impact of combined library/vendor behavior on rejection rates. The vendor chooses the titles which it supplies, and the library determines those it will reject. The rejection rate we observe is as much due to the library's internal funding policies and selection practices as it is to the vendor's choice of titles to ship. Unless the extent to which the library's behavior affects the observed rate is known, the rejection rate is, at best, a measure of library/vendor communication.

The library's behavior can have similar impacts on observed performance in other areas as well. Evans and Argyres in their study of approval plan performance conclude that, even when carefully monitored, approval plans add more unused material than do either librarian selection or faculty selection.[24] This conclusion suggests that librarians at the reporting libraries select more carefully and thoughtfully from other selection tools than they do with book in hand. Who then is responsible for the observed non-use of approval plan additions to the collection, the library or the vendor?

6. *Despite apparent consensus on important performance criteria, there are no standards or norms for approval plan performance.*

In the literature of approval plans, performance criteria are generally listed as advantages or disadvantages that libraries might expect to experience when an approval plan is instituted. Stated in this way, the performance results are assumed to be either generally favorable or unfavorable to libraries. However, in some instances, one author's advantage becomes another's disadvantage, largely depending upon the context of the library from whose point of view the author is writing. We can remove the apparent conflict by listing advantages and disadvantages together under the umbrella of performance criteria which make no assumptions about the level of performance. The advantages and disadvantages listed in Evans and Argyres fine article[25] form the basis for most of the following criteria:

*Approval Plan Performance*

a. Selection/evaluation precision with book in hand.

b. Use of approval materials added to the collection.

c. The costs and procedural impacts on internal library processing.

d. Use of selector's time.

e. Dependence upon vendor.

f. Access to specialized vendor services.

g. Multiple copy provision.

h. Budgetary impacts on total library allocations.

i. Development and maintenance costs of the plan.

*Vendor Performance*

a. Speed of notification/delivery after publication.

b. Breadth of publisher/subject coverage.

c. Discounts.

d. Knowledge of titles expected to be shipped.

e. Duplication of materials received via other means.

f. Percentage of items returned.

g. Number of items claimed.

h. Quality of statistical/managerial reports.

The performance criteria have been divided to distinguish criteria which apply primarily to the general performance of the plan from those which apply specifically to vendor performance. Unfortunately, widely accepted standards for either set of criteria do not exist. A norm for the percentage of items returned does seem to be emerging. Although at least one source noted that returns of over 30% are reported,[26] most sources suggest that rates of 5--10% typify successful plans.[27,28] Vendors generally indicate that rates of up to 15% are acceptable for new plans but that ongoing plans should have rates closer to 5%.[29]

The consensus regarding return rates does not extend to any of the other criteria. One can speculate that the reason for the lack of standards relates to some of the earlier observations in this paper. Libraries are unique so that the performance level expected by one library cannot be extended to another. Or, the negotiated agreements between libraries and vendors mitigate any general norms. Or, finally, perhaps vendor evaluation itself has not been sufficiently structured to permit the analysis necessary to develop and defend standard levels of performance.

Although the six observations made above are necessary to specify a performance evaluation model, they are not sufficient; measurement, a key element in evaluation, must be addressed.

7. *Even under the best circumstances, measurement is fundamentally imprecise.*

In his *Prediction and Optimal Decision*, C. West Churchman, the noted systems analyst and philosopher, explores the science of measurement. He describes several aspects of measurement important to the appraisal process:

a. The purpose of measurement is to make decisions; it therefore should be evaluated by decision making criteria.

b. Effective measurement requires that the error of measurement also be measured.

c. Determining the accuracy of measurement requires information on its possible deviations from reality.

d. A measurement process may lack accuracy for two reasons: it is not consistent or, though consistent, may not have sufficient accuracy for a specific purpose.[30]

These observations support the view that measurement is first of all part of the decision process and must be structured to assist that process. Second, they establish the inherent imprecision of measurement and the need to determine to what extent it is sufficiently accurate for the decision that must be made.

In our quest for hard data to dispel our dependence on generalized expressions of opinion on approval plans, it is important not to ascribe precision to estimates based upon measurements that are inherently imprecise. The point is that the inherent and undetermined error in the measurement itself may undermine the value of assessing vendor performance on some criteria, unless the measurement process can be controlled to achieve the required level of accuracy.

It is also important to decide early in the evaluation design to what standard will the vendor's performance be compared. Essentially there are three alternatives:

1. Compare the vendor's performance to some well established standard;

2. Compare performance to the performance of its competitors in the same setting; and

3. Compare performance against a target measure to which both library and vendor have previously agreed.

The first of these cannot be used; the lack of existing performance standards has already been noted. The second is possible, providing that the library can either 1) duplicate the precise conditions of the approval plan so that two or more vendors can be compared, or 2) control the performance variations that may be due to differences in the conditions. The third avoids both of these problems but requires that the library determine explicit performance levels which, in its view, define a successful plan. The author favors the third alternative because it permits the greatest local control over performance objectives while minimizing the risk of unfair or inequitable vendor appraisals.

*Specifications for a Vendor Evaluation Model*

The previous section made several observations regarding the special nature of library/vendor relationships in an approval plan context. The underlying concepts of these observations held significant implications for an approval plan vendor evaluation design. From these implications, we can derive a set of basic specifications for an approval plan vendor evaluation model.

1. The design should identify and measure the services which add value to the materials received via the plan.

2. The minimum standard of performance should not be less than the library could achieve by providing these services for itself.

3. The agreement should be a precise, written document which describes mutual responsibilities, benefits, performance expectations, and terms of separation.

4. The design should include steps which identify the library's needs, the performance required of the plan to satisfy those needs, and the performance the library must require of itself.

5. The evaluation process should provide opportunities for regular, frequent vendor-initiated communication and early, systematic library feedback on vendor performance.

6. The evaluation design must acknowledge the duration of the

relationship, testing performance over an extended period of time rather than relying upon a "snapshot" approach.

7. The library must acknowledge its impact on observed measures of overall approval plan performance. It should identify to what extent it coproduces the measure of performance and establish performance levels for itself for these criteria.

8. The design should gear the measurement process to specific preestablished performance expectations and predetermined decision thresholds, e.g., expected quantities of materials shipped and decisions regarding publisher exclusions and subject scope.

9. The library should determine in advance the accuracy required for each performance criterion. The measurement process should itself be evaluated to determine if it yields enough useful information to be worth its cost to the library.

*A Model for Approval Plan Vendor Evaluation*

The preceding section listed design specifications derived from observations on the special nature of the library/vendor relationship in an approval plan context. This section develops a model for an approval plan vendor evaluation process which is composed of five stages, some of which may be repeated depending upon the decision reached at the conclusion of each evaluation cycle. Diagram I illustrates the process. The discussion which follows describes each of the five stages, linking the description to earlier observations and giving examples where appropriate.

*1. Vendor Selection*

The foundation for fair and equitable approval vendor evaluation is built during the initial stages of the selection process. Berkner suggests that the development of an approval plan begin with an institutional self-study which analyzes its curricula, clients, materials budget, collection priorities, presents selection tools, staffing, etc.[31] Reidelbach and Shirk recommend that libraries prepare written objectives for the plan and specify its required and desirable features at the outset.[32]

The present study suggests that the library also identify the services provided by the vendor that, in the view of the library, add to the value of materials received via the plan. Examples of such services are the following:

DIAGRAM I

Approval Plan Vendor Evaluation

A Process Model

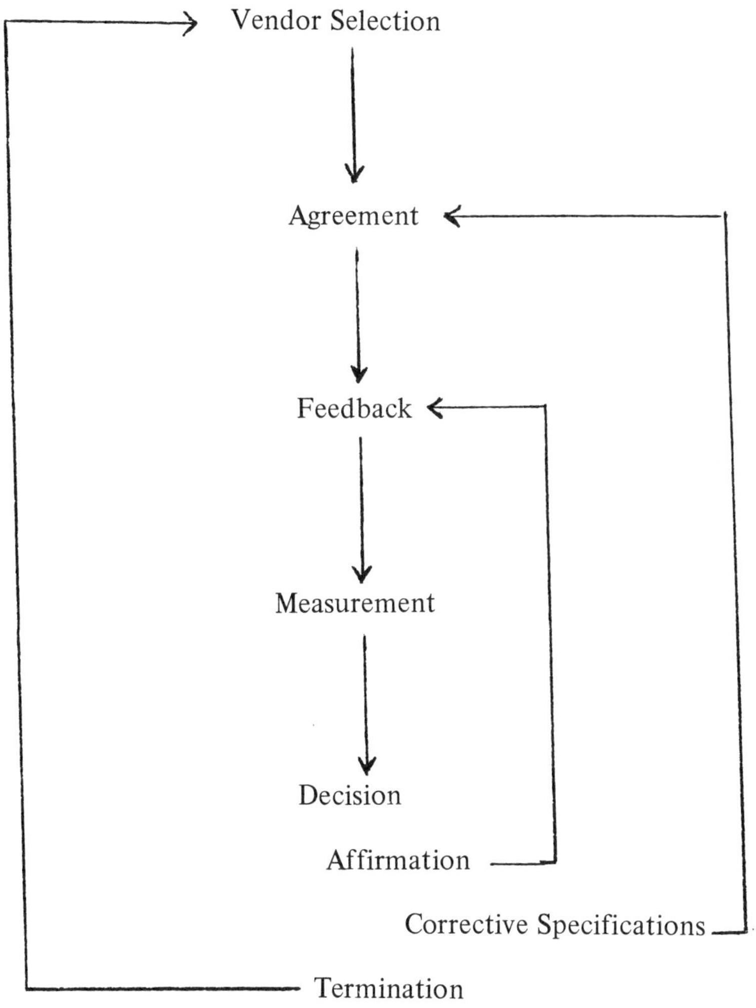

a. Monitoring the output of 4,000–10,000 publishers.

b. Claiming expected materials from publishers.

c. Providing printed bibliographic data with the books as they are shipped.

d. Providing preprinted "instant" credit memos to accompany returns.

e. Maintaining statistics on shipped materials.

The point of identifying these important services early in the selection process is to broaden the basis of selection to cover all areas of importance to the eventual performance of the approval plan.

For similar reasons, it is important to develop during the initial preparation process the vendor performance criteria which will figure prominently in later evaluations. There are two principal reasons for this: 1) the library will be forced to come to terms with its value structure, i.e., what is really important to it; and 2) prospective vendors will be able to advise the library on the extent to which they believe they can satisfy the library's expectations. It also gives the vendor the opportunity to discuss and possibly influence changes in some performance expectations.

During the initial preparation stages, it is desirable to specify expected ranges of performance based, perhaps, on the experience of similar libraries. It is also useful to list the performance criteria roughly in their order of importance to the library. For example . . .

a. Notification slips or books should be shipped between two weeks and two months following publication.

b. Rejections are expected to be between 5% and 20% in the first year of operation.

c. Net discounts (after shipping and service charges when applicable) from total invoice list price should be in the range of 5% to 20%.

d. Claims for expected but not received titles should be in the range of 5% to 15% of the titles shipped the first year of operation.

These parameters are broad enough to open discussions with vendors and prepare the selected vendor to negotiate more specific performance expectations when the approval plan agreement is drafted. Libraries should expect to moderate some performance expectations in exchange for specialized services. Moreover, the ranges provide for variations among vendors. It is reasonable to expect that all vendors, for reasons of their own internal policies and organization, will be able to assure higher levels of performance in some areas than in others. At the point of selection, the library will be able to make its choice based upon the vendor's performance estimates across the full range of criteria. During evaluation the library will then have had the benefit of the vendor's assurances and can legitimately hold the vendor to those assurances.

*2. Agreement*

An earlier section made the observation that an approval plan agreement, regardless of its formality, constituted a contract. However, the word "contract" often conjures the image of lawyers toiling over arcane language. This is not intended. Rather what is needed is an explicit, written, mutually understood agreement which regulates not only the services that the vendor provides to the library but the obligations acknowledged by the library.

This stage in the evaluation process builds upon the foundation erected in stage one. The vendor has been selected upon the basis of its assurances that it could provide a plan that would satisfy the library's primary objectives. The vendor has also demonstrated the ability (or willingness) to perform within performance ranges set by the library. The "contract" or agreement is then the vehicle to clarify the mutual understanding reached by the library and vendor.

Biblarz recommends a formal, written agreement which includes ten elements:[33]

1. Definition of the scope of the plan.

2. Stipulation of expected subject coverage.

3. Establishment of the imprint date for which shipments will begin.

4. Budget allocation for the plan.

5. Conditions regulating return privileges.

6. Service options available through the plan.

7. Frequency of shipments.

8. Type of billing for the plan.

9. Amount of discount or service charges.

10. Terms governing the plan's termination.

To these should be added explicit statements of performance expectations, narrowing the performance ranges used during the vendor selection stage. Generalized expectations based upon the experiences of other libraries are no longer valuable. The library must determine and make explicit the minimum performance levels under which it would require remedial action and perhaps terminate the plan. At the agreement stage, the vendor should be prepared to assure minimum performance levels, given the same assurances that the library will fulfill its responsibilities.

Vendor performance measures at this point should include both explicit statements of the expectations and their weight in an overall judgment of performance. The following example narrows the ranges proposed at the selection stage and weights their importance to the total evaluation:

| *Weight* | | *Performance Measure* |
|---|---|---|
| .40 | a. | Eighty percent (80%) of books or notifications slips should be shipped no later than one month following publication. |
| .30 | b. | Rejection rates should not exceed 15% in the first year of operation. (The library assures that it will accept all materials that comply with the profile. It will also provide an explicit rationale for each rejection.) |
| .20 | c. | Net discounts, adjusted for any service charges or transportation costs, should average 9% in the first year. (This figure recognizes the presses, subjects, and non-subject treatments included as part of the plan.) |
| .05 | d. | Claims for expected but not received titles should not exceed 12% of titles shipped the first year. |
| .05 | e. | Vendor initiated contacts in the first year should average one per week. |
| 1.00 | | TOTAL WEIGHT |

Performance measures such as these make it clear to the vendor that the library will determine its overall performance evaluation based largely upon two factors: prompt fulfillment and precision in its selection of titles for the plan. In libraries with different priorities, other performance criteria, levels of performance, and weights might be listed. Also, as conditions change, the library and the vendor may mutually agree to make changes in performance criteria as well. The most important aspect is that both library and vendor have the opportunity to discuss the criteria and reach mutual agreement. If such measures were incorporated into the agreement, before the operation of the plan began, the library should expect corrective actions if the vendor does not perform as agreed, and the vendor should expect a continuing business relationship if the firm performs as promised.

### *3. Feedback*

The ultimate purpose of approval plan vendor performance evaluation is not to test the vendor but to structure an ongoing, formal dialog intended to improve the utility of the plan to the library. Nevertheless, neither library nor vendor should assume that once an agreement is signed the need to perform as stipulated is a matter for mere discussion. Evaluation would be ineffective if not linked to the potential discovery of needed and *required* changes in either the library's or the vendor's performance.

As we have observed earlier in this paper, the complexity of the approval plan relationship creates the need for early, frequent communication. This is particularly useful when the plan first begins to operate. This is supported by Biblarz's observation that it is important for libraries to express their needs clearly from the outset to be sure their instructions are well understood.[34] The feedback stage in the evaluation model provides this opportunity. Early in the plan's operation, the library and vendor can make minor adjustments in interpretation which will assure the plan is understood similarly by both parties.

But, as Daniel Melcher sagely noted over a decade ago, continuing refinement of the library's instructions is needed to develop a successful approval plan.[35] The model suggested in this paper therefore offers both the opportunity of early, informal feedback on which to base minor adjustments and a more formal appraisal when significant changes are needed.

To increase its usefulness, feedback should be linked to the profile and performance criteria as defined in the agreement. General comments are not valuable; effective feedback should, therefore, have the following characteristics:

1. It should be specific and supported by examples that illustrate the problem.

2. It should be funneled through a single individual who assumes the responsibility for the quality of communication between the library and the vendor.

3. It should acknowledge the library's impact on observed performance and should specify the changes the library is making to improve.

4. It should be frequent and systematic.

5. It should identify desirable or acceptable solutions to problems.

6. It should note successes as well as failures.

*4. Measurement*

Formal measurement and analysis should begin when two conditions are met: first, the plan has been in operation long enough to reach the intended number of shipped material (often six months to a year, depending upon the point in the publishing cycle at which the plan begins); and second, the library and vendor agree that they generally share the same interpretation of the profile and other instructions. Unlike feedback, the measurement stage is a strictly formal process which assesses vendor performance only upon those performance measures to which both parties have previously reached agreement.

Recognizing the inherent imprecision of measurement techniques and the special problems of some performance criteria, it is useful to have incorporated the method of measurement into the initial agreement. For example, delivery speed is an inherently weak performance criterion because fixing publishing date can be so difficult; yet, in the section on agreement it has been listed as follows because of its critical importance to the plan:

> Eighty percent (80%) of books or notification slips should be shipped no later than one month following publication.

The weakness of the performance measure can be partially overcome if both parties agree to a reasonable basis for establishing publication date, e.g., appearance in *Weekly Record*. Although an accurate estimate is desirable, it is not critical if both agree to the source and can accept its level of accuracy. In this instance, both parties would agree that, for the decisions to be determined by this measure, the accuracy of the source is sufficient.

It was also noted in an earlier section that evaluation design should acknowledge that the plan operates over a long period of time. The measurement techniques should therefore accommodate this concern by collecting data over the entire period being reviewed. In the case of new plans, the first six months will probably not yield accurate information because many adjustments in interpretation typically take place during these months. As a consequence, a formal evaluation of vendor performance may not be possible until at least a year of operation has been completed.

If inferences are based upon statistical estimates, it is best to compare the entire confidence interval to the agreed upon performance level. It is risky to make decisions with costly consequences to both library and vendor from data with frequently large variances.

It is also generally useful for a library to examine closely what sort of contribution, positive or negative, it may have unwittingly made to the vendor's observed performance. For example, if the library's procedures date incoming material when the invoice is authorized for payment rather than when it arrives in the shipping room, the observed performance of the vendor will not be as good as it migh have been otherwise. More subtly, it is important to recognize how library controlled changes during the review period may have influenced apparently unrelated performance measures, e.g., a change from block funding of the plan to individual subject funds may increase the rejection rate more than any actions attributable to the vendor.

*5. Decision*

When the measurement and analysis are complete, the library can decide to take one of three actions: affirm that required performance levels are being met by the vendor; specify corrective actions that either the library or vendor must take to make the plan successful; or terminate the agreement. The decision that the library reaches should not be a surprise. The consequences of a positive or negative overall performance appraisal should have been discussed at the time the approval plan agreement was drafted, particularly in the section regarding termination of the plan.

If performance meets or exceeds performance levels specified for each criterion, affirmation of the plan should be expected, provided that funds remain to support it. The initial efforts of both parties have been successful, and the agreement is renewed. This, of course, does not mean that there should not be adjustments to the profile or performance standards to reflect changing needs. It means that the vendor has satisfied the performance requirements and deserves the library's continued loyalty.

If the vendor's performance does not satisfy all the criteria, the library should specify the required changes in performance, the period set aside for corrective action, and the time at which the next formal evaluation will take place. If observed failure to reach agreed upon performance levels is due to the library, it must assess its ability to make the changes necessary to the plan's success. Reassessment is just as critical in this case as it is when the vendor is not performing. If the plan is not satisfying required performance levels, its continuation compounds the costs in lost staff time, organizational energy, and money.[36]

The evaluation model presented in this paper recommends that the first formal evaluation not result in a decision to terminate the approval plan. It recommends, rather, that the evaluation process complete the cycle at least a second time while corrective actions are taken. This recommendation emerges from the observation of the complexity of the approval plan relationship, the joint responsibility of the library and the vendor to do what they can to make the plan work, and the cost to both parties should the plan be terminated. However, it should be clear to the vendor that termination is the likely result if the corrective actions taken by *either* the vendor or the library are not successful. It is the nature of the relationship that the vendor suffers in either case. The vendor should have, however, the assurance that another dealer will not benefit from their loss if the library cannot fulfill its responsibilities.

### *Summary*

This paper develops a rationale for an approval plan vendor performance evaluation model based upon observations of the special relationships between library and vendor that approval plans create. Key among these observations is that the library, in many respects, coproduces commonly observed performance measures and must, therefore, control the impact of its behavior when doing an evaluation. A five-stage evaluation process is suggested which begins prior to vendor selection, incorporates extensive feedback, and extends to the potential termination of the approval agreement.

## Notes

1. Jan Gregor and Wendy Carol Fraser, "A University of Windsor Experience with an Approval Plan in Three Subjects and Three Vendors." *Canadian Library Journal* 38:227–231 (August 1981).

2. Linda Ann Hulbert and David Stewart Curry, "Evaluation of an Approval Plan," *College and Research Libraries* 39:485--491 (November 1978).

3. Thomas W. Leonhardt, "An Approval Plan: How It Failed, How It Could Succeed: A Case Study of the Boise State University Library," in International Conference of Approval Plans and Collection Development, 4th, Milwaukee, 1979, *Shaping Library Collections for the 1980's*, (Phoenix: Oryx Press, 1980) p.69--73.

4. American Library Association, Resources and Technical Services Division, Resources Section, Collection Management and Development Committee, *Guidelines for Evaluating Performance of Vendors for In-print Monographs*, (Fifth Revised Draft: January 1984).

5. Milton T. Wolf, "Approval Plans: A Paradigm of Library Economics," in International Conference of Approval Plans and Collection Development, 4th, Milwaukee, 1979, *Shaping Library Collections for the 1980's*, (Phoenix: Oryx Press, 1980) p.182.

6. Kathleen McCullough, Edwin D. Posey and Doyle C. Pickett, *Approval Plans and Academic Libraries: An Interpretive Survey*, (Phoenix: Oryx Press, 1977) p.123.

7. Lawrence M. Friedman, *Contract Law in America: A Social and Economic Case Study*, (Madison and Milwaukee: University of Wisconsin Press, 1965) p.15.

8. Friedman, *Contract Law*, p.17.

9. Jennifer S. Cargill and Brian Alley, *Practical Approval Plan Management*, (Phoenix: Oryx Press, 1979) p.31.

10. Dora Biblarz, "Special Emphasis Acquisitions Plans," in International Conference of Approval Plans and Collection Development, 4th, Milwaukee, 1979, *Shaping Library Collections for the 1980's*, (Phoenix: Oryx Press, 1980) p.84.

11. Paul H. Mosher, "Waiting for Godot: Rating Approval Service Vendors," in International Conference of Approval Plans and Collection Development, 4th, Milwaukee, 1979, *Shaping Library Collections for the 1980's*, (Phoenix: Oryx Press, 1980) p.160.

12. McCullough, Posey, and Pickett, *Approval Plans*, p.129--130.

13. John H. Reidelbach and Gary M. Shirk, "Selecting an Approval Plan Vendor: Comparative Vendor Data," (publication in progress).

14. Biblarz, "Special Emphasis," p.87.

15. Sharon Bonk and Mina B. LaCroix, "Approval Plans in a Developing University Library 1970–79: A Case Study," in International Conference of Approval Plans and Collection Development, 4th, Milwaukee, 1979, *Shaping Library Collections for the 1980's*, (Phoenix: Oryx Press, 1980) p.39.

16. Cargill and Alley, *Practical Approval Plan Management*, p.39.

17. McCullough, Posey, and Pickett, *Approval Plans*, p.143.

18. G. Edward Evans and Claudia White Argyres, "Approval Plans and Collection Development in Academic Libraries," *Library Resources and Technical Services* 18(1):38 (Winter 1974).

19. Gregor and Fraser, "A University of Windsor Experience," p.228.

20. Donald G. Stave, "Approval Book Acquisition: Some Vendor Requirements and Practices," in International Conference of Approval Plans and Collection Development, 4th, Milwaukee, 1979, *Shaping Library Collections for the 1980's*, (Phoenix: Oryx Press, 1980) p.135.

21. Cargill and Alley, *Practical Approval Plan Management*, p.25.

22. Cargill and Alley, *Practical Approval Plan Management*, p.23.

23. Gregor and Fraser, "A University of Windsor Experience," p.230.

24. Evans and Argyres, "Approval Plans and Collection Development," p.50.

25. Evans and Argyres, "Approval Plans and Collection Development," p.35--50.

26. Cargill and Alley, *Practical Approval Plan Management*, p26.

27. Gregor and Fraser, "A University of Windsor Experience," p229.

28. Evans and Argyres, "Approval Plans and Collection Development," p.38.

29. Reidelbach and Shirk, "Comparative Vendor Data."

30. C. West Churchman, *Prediction and Optimal Decision: Philosophical Issues of a Science of Values*, (Englewood Cliffs, NJ: Prentice-Hall, 1961) p.101–128.

31. Dimity S. Berkner, "Considerations in Selecting an Approval Plan," in International Conference of Approval Plans and Collection Development, 4th, Milwaukee, 1979, *Shaping Library Collections for the 1980's*, (Phoenix: Oryx Press, 1980), p144--146.

32. John H. Reidelbach and Gary M. Shirk, "Selecting an Approval Plan Vendor: A Step-by-Step Process," *Library Acquisitions: Practice and Theory* 7:116–117 (1983).

33. Biblarz, "Special Emphasis," p.88.

34. Biblarz, "Special Emphasis," p.87.

35. Daniel Melcher, *Melcher on Acquisitions*, (Chicago: American Library Association, 1971) p.110.

36. Biblarz, "Special Emphasis," p.90.

# EVALUATING THE ROLE AND EFFECTIVENESS OF APPROVAL PLANS FOR LIBRARY COLLECTION DEVELOPMENT

by

Stanley P. Hodge

*Introduction*

Despite four international conferences covering all dimensions of approval plans, enormous progress in the sophistication of services by book vendors, and several articles each year devoted to analyzing various facets of approval programs, librarians continue to treat this method of materials acquisition with some degree of ambivalence. Blame it on unrealistic expectations, the anxiety syndrome, poor communication, false promises, or closed minds – there continue to be several shared concerns regarding the role and effectiveness of approval plans as a tool for collection development. As an administrator over what is purported to be the largest single domestic approval plan account in the nation, my colleagues and I have a justifiable concern for the performance of approval programs.

The advantages and disadvantages of approval plans have been well documented in recent literature on the topic.[1-3] This paper will attempt to minimize reiteration and focus instead on the various types of approval plan evaluations, methods to determine problem areas, and descriptions of some studies that relate to the role and effectiveness of approval plans at one institution.

*Types of Approval Plan Evaluations*

Several types of evaluations related to approval plans have been described in the literature. Among their purposes are:

(a) to recommend important criteria applicable in choosing an approval plan vendor;[4-5]

---

The author wishes to express his thanks to Colleen Cook, Judy Droessler, and Michael Nyerges (members of the Ad Hoc Committee on Approval Plan Evaluation) and to Jay Poole, Sara Donaldson, and Dorothy Kelly for their assistance or comments.

(b) to compare concurrently the performance of two or more vendors;[6-7]

(c) to assess how an existing approval plan or plans actually meet a library's needs in specific subject areas;[8-11]

(d) to gauge the effectiveness of approval plans as a method of collection development from several perspectives.[12-13]

This paper is most similar in purpose to the two latter types of approval plan evaluations. In its broader context it consists of a case study that is concerned with: how the relevant questions to be investigated were determined, some research methodologies used to answer those questions, and the place of the Library's approval program in relation to its overall collection development strategy.

Although libraries have different collection development needs, different organizational structures, and different expectations about what their approval plans do, some of Texas A&M University Library's concerns are no doubt shared by others.

A major focus of the evaluation is the effectiveness of a domestic jobber's provision of science and technology material. Other concerns of interest to perhaps a larger audience include the coverage of university press books and the efficiency of approval plans compared to firm order acquisitions.

*Determining Areas of Concern*

When concerns exist about the role and adequacy of approval programs in a library's overall collection development strategy, different methods may be used to elicit those concerns. Thomas Leonhardt,[14] in an effort to examine attitudes toward a faltering approval plan at Boise State University Library, asked those librarians with selection responsibilities a series of fifteen questions. Examples were:

Are you in favor of approval plans?

Do you think our approval plan is effective, marginal, or poor?

Where do approval plan problems exist?

In the Boise State case, different perceptions produced some contradictory answers as well as a variety of proposed solutions to the problems. This exemplifies the complexity of some problems extant in approval programs, including those of communication and varying perceptions.

At Texas A&M University Library, the issue of approval plans surfaced in a nominal group technique session. The NGT, as it is called, is an exercise where library faculty meet in small groups and suggest the important issues confronting the library. The dozens of issues forthcoming from these groups are then synthesized and voted on to produce a list of issues determined to be of most critical concern. Some type of an evaluation of the Library's approval plans was one of several issues that received majority support.

An ad hoc committee was appointed that consisted of a cross-section of four library faculty. The next step was to determine what specific aspects of approval plans were viewed as requiring examination.

Rather than distribute a written survey questionnaire with a series of closed and/or open-ended questions, the committee chair elected to meet with the public and technical service librarians in two separate meetings and engage in a free-for-all discussion about some of their concerns. The intent of this approach was, first, to stimulate thinking through an open exchange of ideas about what the library faculty's concerns and expectations were, and second, to attempt to correct any miconceptions about the approval plans that may have been held. One effect of approval plan evaluations can be the shattering of myths and misunderstandings about what is occurring, or even possible, given the state of the art. This approach appeared to work, for lengthy discussions resulted, and the nature and role of approval plans were clarified.

Five specific topics emerged from these discussions that resulted in a charge to the Ad Hoc Committee on Approval Plan Evaluation. The five topics to be addressed were:

1. Should all the approval plans be continued? Should only certain ones be continued? What justification is there for continuing the plans? Should any of the plans be expanded? For what reasons should they be expanded?

2. Is the domestic approval plan adequate in supplying the essential materials as we currently depend on it?

3. Are the domestic approval plans adequate in supplying those publishers considered essential? Who are the essential publishers?

4. To what extent can the approval plans be relied upon to supply conference proceedings? Should consideration be given to other means of acquiring proceedings?

5. What types of publishers, formats, and which subjects require some mechanism to back up the approval plans? How should such back up procedures be handled?

The Committee was also requested to support their findings with facts and documentation.

*General Description of the Library's Collection Development Activities and the Domestic Approval Plan*

A brief background about the source of monograph materials and the various personnel responsible for collection development at the University Library is appropriate in order to gain a perspective of the approval plans' role in the overall collection development picture.

Ultimate responsibility for collection development lies with the Resource Development Division's librarians – three of whom are assigned broad subject area responsibilities for firm order selection and approval plans. Although all library and teaching faculty may generate requests, most firm order selections are made by resource development and reference librarians. Selection involvement by the teaching faculty is encouraged – especially in their research interest areas but has been uneven and has played an ever diminishing role over the years. Collection policies, which have been drafted for over forty subject areas to date, assist in both the fine tuning of approval plan profiles and in guiding the selection decisions of librarians.

ILLUSTRATION I

Source of Monograph Receipts and Total of Expenditures for 6 Months (Sept., 1982--Feb., 1983)

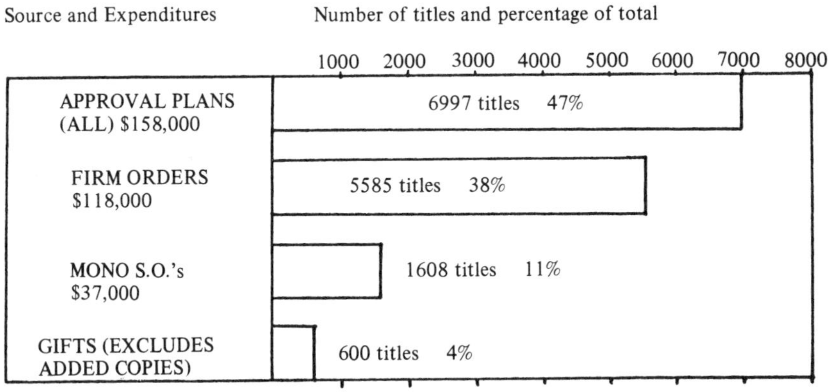

Illustration I indicates that the major sources of current monographs for a selected six-month period were its five approval plans. This included a major plan of a domestic vendor (with a broad subject profile); a British vendor's plan (which supplied books generated from form selections); two scientific publishers' approval plans; and a German language literature and criticism plan. The significance of the domestic approval plan is dramatized by more recent statistics. In calendar year 1983 18,016 books were sent – 2,247 in response to notification slips. There were 1,503 returns, or about eight percent of the receipts. More books were returned as duplicates than as rejects.

Provision of materials through the major domestic plan by broad subject area over the same six-month period is shown in Illustration II.

Since the thrust of Texas A&M's research programs and the majority of its students are engaged in science, engineering, and agriculture, figures on Illustration II indicate why some librarians were concerned with the adequacy of the domestic approval plan in supplying science and technology books. Despite the recognition that serial literature is generally viewed as being more significant than monographs for sci-tech disciplines, in-house use and circulation of science and technology monographs are high.

### *Description of Some Studies Conducted*

In deliberating the five topics that the Ad Hoc Committee was charged to investigate, several studies to assist in providing its evaluation and recommendations were devised. Some of these studies are described as follows.

#### *American Book Publishing Record (ABPR) Study*

Purpose

A study using *ABPR* was conducted in order to determine the Library's receipts of science and technology material listed in this source. The approval plans provision of science and technology material was of particular concern since it was felt that more material should be provided in view of the university's curriculum and research needs. Therefore, one objective of this study was to determine how many and what type of the sci-tech monographs listed in *ABPR* were received on approval plans within a reasonable amount of time. Such an approach also provides a review of what the approval vendors were *not* sending.

ILLUSTRATION II

MAJOR DOMESTIC APPROVAL PLAN RECEIPT SUMMARY
FOR 6 MONTHS (SEPT., 1982 - FEB., 1983)

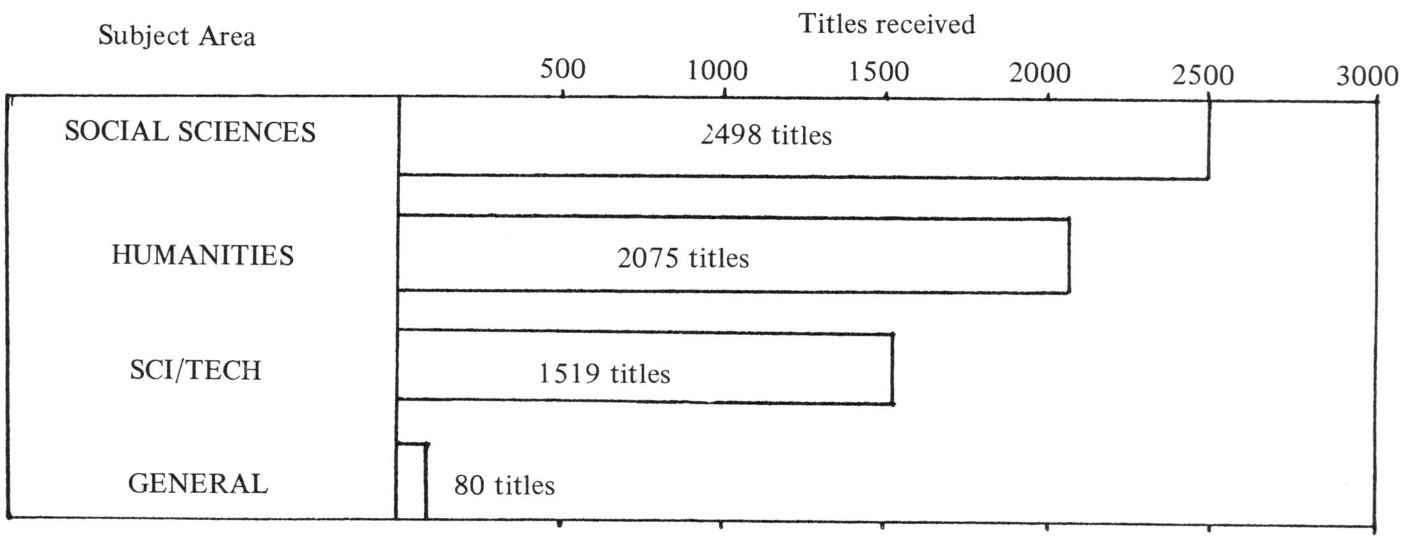

Methodology

The study was conducted in May/June 1983. The December 1982 issue of *ABPR* was selected to use since it was necessary to allow approval plan and firm order selections a chance to be provided after their announcement. Also, many of the citations in *ABPR* are based on cataloging in publication (CIP) information and some of the material was not actually available until months later. Monographs classified in the Dewey numbers 500--609, 620--639, 660--679, and 690--699 were used. The gaps, represented by medicine, 610--619; home economics, 640--649; and industrial arts, 680--689, were not considered crucial to the Library's collection.

TABLE I

*ABPR* Study Overall Results

| | | |
|---|---|---|
| Total S/T Items in Dec. '82 *ABPR* | | 593 |
| Undergraduate Textbooks | 45 | |
| Reprints | 13 | |
| Juvenile Books | 35 | |
| Total Unlikely to be Supplied | 93 | |
| Total Books Eligible for Selection | | 500 |
| Total Held or On Order in June, 1983 (60%) | | 300 |
| Total Received on Approval Plans (69% of those held) (42% of those eligible) | | 208 |
| Domestic Plan | 156 | |
| British Slip Plan | 8 | |
| Elsevier | 23 | |
| Springer-Verlag | 21 | |
| Total Received on Approval Plans | 208 | |
| Total Received Through Firm or Standing Orders (31% of those held) (18% of those eligible) | | 92 |
| Total Not Received Through Any Method (40%) | | 200 |

Five hundred and ninety-three books from over 230 publishers were included in the classifications checked. Of those, ninety-three were identified as likely to be undergraduate textbooks, reprints or juvenile literature – material that is excluded on the Library's book approval plan. This reduced the items to be checked to exactly 500 titles. The approval plan receipt files were checked to identify all items received on an approval plan. Next, the OCLC Acquisitions Subsystem was checked to identify all items on order or received through firm and standing orders. Finally, a check of the public catalog was made of all items not previously indicated as being received or on order.

## Findings

Table I indicates the results of this study. Overall, sixty percent of the eligible items listed in the sci-tech section of *ABPR* were held or on order six months after the appearance of the issue. Of the 300 items held, 208 or 69% had been received on approval plans and 31% had been received as a result of a firm or standing order. Two hundred items, or 40% had been neither received nor ordered. In addition, a check for the total eligible titles held and the method of receipt was made by subject area. This is illustrated in Table II.

TABLE II

*ABPR* Study Results By Subject

| Subject | Eligible Titles Listed | Titles Held | % | Rcvd. on Appr. | % of Receipts on Appr. | % Eligible Titles Recvd. on Appr. |
|---|---|---|---|---|---|---|
| Gen.Sci. & Math | 75 | 50 | 67 | 43 | 86 | 57 |
| Chemistry | 25 | 22 | 88 | 13 | 59 | 52 |
| Tech. & Eng. | 133 | 79 | 59 | 60 | 76 | 45 |
| Astronomy & Physics | 35 | 25 | 71 | 15 | 60 | 43 |
| Chem. Tech. | 33 | 19 | 58 | 14 | 74 | 42 |
| Biol. Sci. | 96 | 51 | 52 | 37 | 73 | 39 |
| Agr., Animal Sci.,Vet.Sci. | 42 | 22 | 52 | 12 | 55 | 29 |
| Manufactrng | 8 | 4 | 50 | 2 | 50 | 25 |
| Geoscis. | 33 | 19 | 56 | 8 | 42 | 24 |
| Build.Constr. | 20 | 9 | 45 | 4 | 44 | 20 |
| TOTALS: | 500 | 300 | 60% | 208 | 69% | 42% |

The percentage of titles held varied from 45% in building construction up to 88% in chemistry. Approval plans supplied only 42% and 44% of the titles held in geosciences and building construction respectively, but 86% of the general science and mathematics books held were supplied on approval.

The study indicates that while only 42% of the eligible sci-tech books are supplied on approval to the Library six months after their inclusion in *ABPR*, the approval plans are still supplying over two-thirds of the sci-tech material (69%) received by that time. Many of the remaining 31% received are part of a numbered series on standing order and are intentionally excluded from the approval profile.

What of the 40% of potentially eligible items which had not been received at all? Examination of the citations indicated that the likely reasons for non-receipt on approval were:

1. Books with CIP entries may not yet have been published or were supplied later. Some are claimed on the approval plan.

2. Small or non-trade publishers were not as well covered, or not covered in as timely a manner, by the domestic approval vendor.

3. The material may not have been included in the Library's approval book profile, e.g., it was categorized by a modifier that was excluded entirely, or notification was provided by means of a slip, but not selected.

   This is particularly the case with some of the engineering areas in Dewey classes 620--629 where there are many "marginal" examples, such as *Takeoffs and Touchdowns: My Sixty Years of Flying, Emergency Service Vehicles of the U.K.*, and numerous automobile and motorcycle repair manuals.

Still, the approval plans appear to be supplying automatically a large portion of the more academically-oriented, higher quality books of the major sci-tech publishers in a timely manner.

## Recommendations

Obviously, approval plans will not supply *all* books that will be selected by faculty, nor should they be expected to. However, some general recommendations for effectively monitoring approval plans in the scientific and technology areas would be:

1. Wait at least four to six months after *ABPR* is issued to monitor approval receipts since many citations are based on CIP information and the material will not be available for distribution when *ABPR* is issued.

2. While monitoring an approval plan on a title-by-title basis defeats several of the plan's inherent advantages, certain subject areas appear either to have more items which fall into marginal categories on the approval profile or include a greater proportion of books from non-trade publishers and be less comprehensively covered. Consequently, a lower percentage of books in those subjects will be provided on approval plans. Examples are manufacturing, building construction, agriculture, and geosciences. Books in these subjects should be closely monitored with publisher's catalogs from scholarly societies, institutes, associations, etc., as well as with *ABPR*.

3. Periodical checks of review sources, e.g., *Choice* and *New Technical Books*, will help ensure eventual awareness of highly regarded and important sci-tech works that may have been missed due to the Library's profile, or by the approval vendor.

### *Interlibrary Loan Study*

#### Purpose

Interlibrary loan requests reflect those research needs of graduate students and faculty which were unmet by the Library's collection. Although journal articles comprise the bulk of a large interlibrary loan operation, (7,333 fulfilled requests in fiscal year 1983 for all categories of material), an analysis of requests for recently published monographs might reveal some general characteristics about the needs of the Library's clientele and suggest selection strategies that might ameliorate some of the collection's weak areas.

#### Methodology

Requests for monographs processed by the Interlibrary Service Division from January through April 1983 were analyzed by subject and type of publisher. Monograph requests reflecting only imprints published since 1973 were examined in order to cover the approximate period that domestic approval plans had been in place. Nearly 280 OCLC Interlibrary Loan Subsystem printouts were converted to the full MARC record for use in this study. The requests were analyzed by:

ILLUSTRATION III

INTERLIBRARY LOAN REQUESTS BY BROAD SUBJECT AREA AND SUBJECTS (LC CLASS NUMBER) MOST HIGHLY REQUESTED

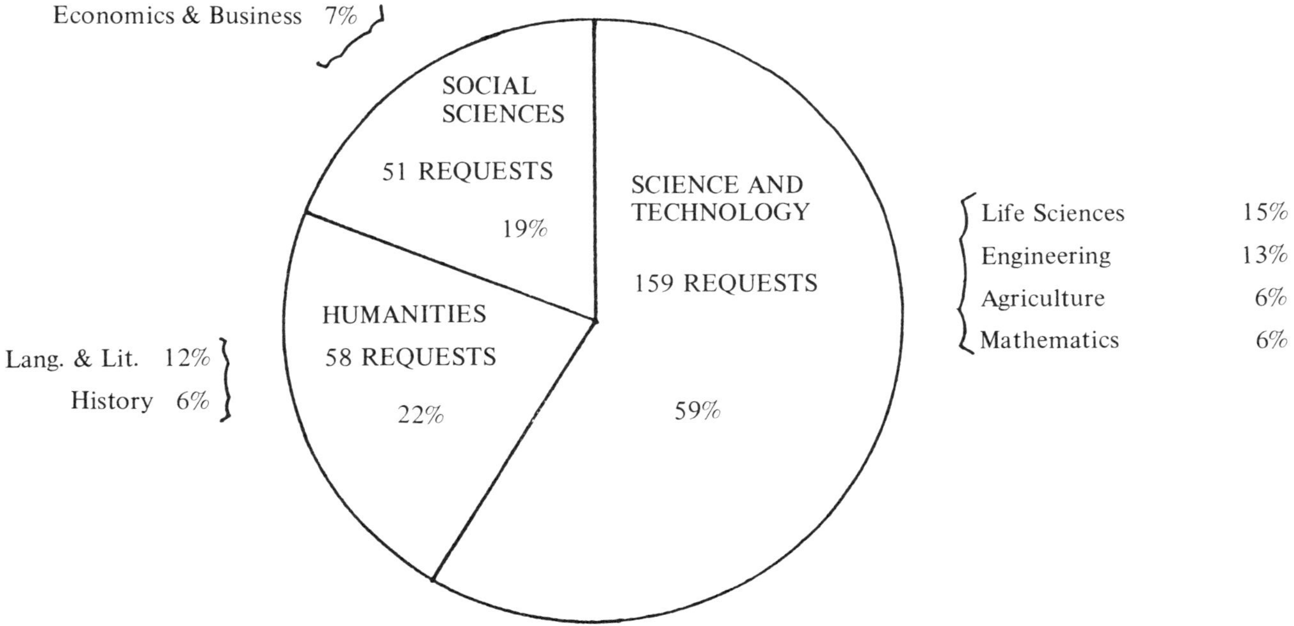

ILLUSTRATION IV

UNIVERSITY PRESS BOOKS SUPPLIED TO TEXAS A&M UNIV. LIBRARY ON APPROVAL, SEPT. - DEC., 1982 (1550 TITLES)

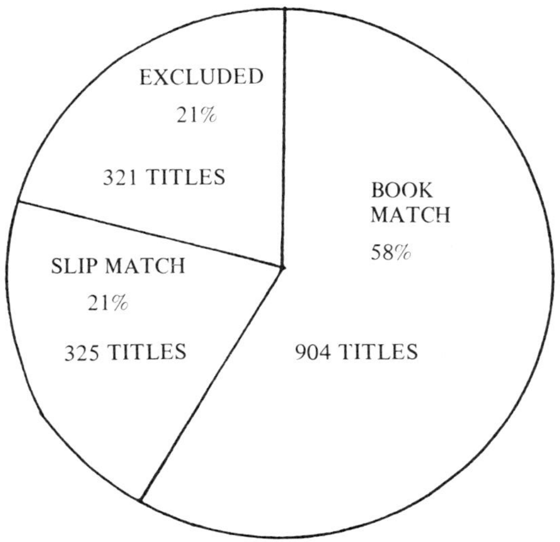


REASONS FOR EXCLUSION: Continuations, books in sets, "general supplementary" books, local emphasis (particularly for music, history and religion), clinical medicine topics, publication date cutoff to exclude 1981 imprints.

1. Broad subject area, e.g., humanities, social sciences, science and technology, and by LC class numbers;

2. Type of publisher, e.g., commercial, society or association, government agency, university press; and,

3. Foreign or domestic imprint.

Findings

1. Subject Analysis

The largest proportion of requests (59%) pertained to science and technology subjects. Within this area books in the life sciences (classes QH-QR) were requested most frequently. This classification was followed by requests for materials in engineering, agriculture, mathematics, medicine, and geology.

Twenty-two percent of the total number of requests were for materials in the humanities. Books on language and literature were requested most frequently, and a relatively large number of requests was also received for history books.

Requests for social science books accounted for 19% of the total, with business and sociology materials being most in demand.

Texas A&M's curricular and research interests and the fact that only monographs published since 1973 were analyzed would partially explain the preponderance of science and technology requests since currency of information is less crucial in the humanities and social sciences.

TABLE III

I.L.L. Monograph Requests by Type of Publisher

| Type | U.S. | Foreign | Total | Percentage |
|---|---|---|---|---|
| Commercial | 110 | 58 | 168 | 61% |
| Institutes, Univ. Depts. | 29 | 20 | 49 | 18% |
| Societies, Associations | ---- | ---- | 30 | 11% |
| Government Publications | 18 | 2 | 20 | 7% |
| University Presses | 7 | 3 | 10 | 3+% |
| TOTAL | | | 277 | 100% |

50 titles or 18% of requests were for proceedings of conferences.

2. Publisher Analysis

Sixty-one percent of the requests examined were for books published by commercial houses. Publications of domestic commercial publishers were requested nearly twice as often as those of foreign commercial publishers. Major science publishers (e.g., Wiley, Plenum, Springer-Verlag, and Elsevier) were well represented in this sample.

Requests for publications of institutes, museums, and university departments accounted for 18% of the materials requested.

Nearly 11% of the total number of requests were for books of professional or scholarly societies and associations which were heavily skewed toward the science and technology fields. Of the remaining publisher categories, government agencies (primarily federal) accounted for 7% while university press books were requested least often – less than 4% of the total.

3. Domestic – Foreign Imprint Analysis

Overall, foreign imprints accounted for one-third of the requests submitted. No analysis by country of origin or language was conducted, however. Although unrelated to any of the above three categories of analysis, it was also observed that nearly 20% or fifty titles were for proceedings of conferences.

Recommendations

The interlibrary loan study produced a few surprises and indicates that if more improvements in the research collection are to be made, some subjects and types of publications require additional attention and collection mechanisms beyond a reliance on approval programs and the Library's other selection methods. It should also be stressed that some items are not "good bets" to be acquired and are more suitably dealt with through a network of library resources sharing activities and practices – interlibrary loan being one of them.

As a type-of-use study, the ILL analysis indicated that, "monographically speaking," the emphasis on acquisition of current imprints for those engaged in scientific and technological research needs to be continued, if not intensified; that commercially published books are heavily requested vis-a-vis non-commercial publications; that relevant foreign publications and conference proceedings could be more actively pursued; and finally, that government documents (outside of the U.S. federal category) and university press publications are not a critical weakness.

## *University Press Publications Study*

### Purpose

A frequent question asked by teaching faculty at Texas A&M University is: "Does the Library receive all university press books?" About 4,000 university press titles are published or distributed in the U.S. each year. Attitudes differ among teaching and library faculty on whether all or only selected university press books should be acquired. When the Ad Hoc Committee began its work, no current information was available regarding the adequacy of the domestic approval plan's coverage of university presses. Since the major burden of current university press coverage fell on the domestic approval plan, the object of the study was to determine the extent to which university press books were supplied on approval and whether those items excluded constituted a serious oversight.

### Methodology

The methodology employed provides a good example of how a vendor's automated records can be used to advantage in evaluating certain dimensions of an approval program. The domestic approval plan vendor supplied a listing of all university press titles handled and indicated those supplied to the Library for the four-month period September–December 1982. This listing represented about one-third the annual output of all university press books published or distributed in the U.S. These data were furnished on a printout together with a notation on whether there was a "book-match," "slip-match," or an exclusion due to the profile. The listings were arranged so possible publisher patterns might be discerned. Overall totals were compiled, observations made about the types of books being excluded, and findings noted.

### Findings

The vendor listed 1,550 university press books in its approval plan coverage for the four-month period. This included foreign imprints distributed in the U.S., i.e., Aberdeen, Australian National University, British Columbia, etc. Overall results are shown in Illustration IV.

A few observations were made while perusing the 1,500 titles: local history was a major factor for slip rather than book matches. This is especially true of presses, e.g., Arizona, Kentucky, and Nebraska, which devote much of their efforts to state and regionally-oriented works. Presses such as Chicago and Harvard had a higher book-match percentage since their material was of interest to a wider audience. Another reason for non-book matches was the large number of reprints which, if they fit the subject parameters, were automatically supplied on slips. One area of concern, however, was the number of 1981 imprints which were being shipped by the vendor during late 1982 but were excluded since the Library's instructions to the vendor were to disregard a prior year's imprints after September of the current year.

Recommendations

Although nearly 80 percent of university press titles are supplied on approval or alerted by slip matches, the concern among certain segments of the faculty suggests that further precautions be made to increase the reliability of university press coverage. These changes are already in place. First, some local history categories were changed from slip to book provision on the basis of the History Department's collection development policy. Second, a separate account covering only university press books was established to permit items previously excluded by certain modifiers to become slip notifications. Thus, the Library is now sent either a book or slip for *all* university press items.

This type of arrangement might also be advantageously applied to imprints of other publishers that a library views as crucial but would not collect comprehensively. The drawback of over-reliance on a slip notification arrangement, whether vendor or library regulated, is that non-returnable books falling in marginal areas will be chosen on the basis of the slip's bibliographical information rather than from an examination of the book itself. This is similar to selecting from *ABPR*; and while it reduces the return rate of inappropriate material, books selected from slips are also delayed in their receipt.

## *Other Studies Conducted*

### *Conference Proceedings Study*

Two additional studies will also be mentioned but covered in less detail than the others. When approval plan evaluations are conducted, some attention should be centered on those types of material which are perceived as weak areas of coverage. In this case, several librarians not only considered conference proceedings to be superficially covered by approval plans, but they viewed the entire selection process with regard to this format as a weak area in the Library's collection development strategy.

Conference Proceedings are frequently cited by scientists as a preferred information source second only to journals in importance. Although several bibliographic tools exist to help librarians select, verify, and order them, acquiring these reports of meetings and presentations can still be a formidable chore. Conference proceedings may be acquired as part of an approval plan (usually as non-returnable items alerted by means of form selections) but most require a more active approach such as: (1) contacting a conference sponsor regarding publication plans, (2) selecting from a specialized bibliographic tool, or (3) placing a standing order.[15]

The Committee's objectives in the conference proceedings study were to determine the number of sci-tech proceedings being acquired and the major avenues of their receipt. An issue of Interdok's *Directory of Published Proceedings: Series SEMT* was checked for holdings and, when possible, for source of supply to the Library. All 336 citations in the issue were examined. Fifty were eliminated from consideration because they dealt with medicine or were considered inappropriate for the collection. Overall, the Library held 57% of the 286 titles considered potentially useful. The major source of these proceedings was via standing or blanket orders (42% of those held). Thirty-five percent of those acquired were received through the NTIS depository plans.

When it is necessary to "work backward" in a study, it is sometimes discovered that some kinds of data that would have been useful are unfortunately not available. In this instance it could not be determined in all cases from the Library's records whether the remaining 23% of those proceedings held were acquired through approval plans or firm orders. Nevertheless, it came as no surprise to most that approval plans were probably supplying only between 10–20% of the proceedings the Library acquired.

Given the Library's present reliance on standing orders, it would be unlikely that approval plan profile adjustments would significantly increase the acquisition rate of this elusive and troublesome type of format should more complete coverage of proceedings be desired. Clearly, if most of the estimated 3,000 potentially useful sci-tech proceedings listed in the *Directory* each year were to be acquired, additional and different strategies would have to be employed, and some of these alternatives were suggested by the committee.

### *Staff Requirements Study*

One frequently cited advantage of collection development through approval plans is the alleged economy compared to placing firm order acquisitions. Cost studies may involve only a few or several considerations. In this case, a relatively simple comparison was made of the number of classified staff required to perform the technical operations in both types of processes. The personnel requirements of two of the Library's Divisions were studied. Table IV outlines the situation.

TABLE IV

Classified Staff Requirements for Processing Approval Books and Firm Orders

| | Acquisitions Division | Resource Development Division |
|---|---|---|
| Approval Plan Functions: | None | Sorting and distributing slips; Approval claims; Receiving and displaying books; Pre-catalog searching; Processing invoices |
| Classified Staff Assigned: | None | 3.0 FTE |

F.Y. 1983: 14,800 books/3.0 FTE = 4,933 books per position for approval books.

**********

| | | |
|---|---|---|
| Firm Order Functions: | Assigning vendor<br>Ordering on OCLC Subsystem<br>Receiving on OCLC Subsystem<br>Fund expenditure<br>Processing invoices<br>Claiming | Bibliographic checks for selections<br>Pre-order searching<br>Pre-catalog searching<br>& cancelling |
| Classified Staff Assigned: | 5.5 FTE | 3.5 FTE |

F.Y. 1983: 12,000 books/9.0 FTE = 1,333 books per position for firm orders.

Although this study ignores the function of librarians who must in both cases perform selection responsibilities, and supervise and assist staff, the time devoted to firm order selection has always been greater than for approval plan administration. Granted, a large number of the firm orders are hard-to-get or "garbage" orders as some vendors describe them; but if approval plans will supply the majority of orders in a more cost effective manner, the Library cannot ignore the economic implications.

*Conclusion*

The evaluations described in this paper have provided some specific results related to the subject areas, types of publishers, and formats which are well or inadequately served by one library's approval plans. In some cases, the librarian's anxiety may be relieved by communicating concerns to the vendors' representatives. Representatives will usually know whether profile adjustments will rectify any problem areas which are identified. (The university press example described in this paper is one instance.) However, an evaluation and follow up with the vendor may reveal that an adjustment to the profile will not necessarily resolve certain types of problems, and other corrective measures must be pursued. (This is the likely situation in the conference proceedings study.) In either case, approval plan evaluations may isolate some specific problem areas which will inform those persons charged with collection development responsibilities about areas which need more attention.

Approval plans may be analyzed in many ways. Only a few of their aspects were described in this paper. Other possibilities include time, cost and service studies, and comparisons of alternative procedures for processing approval shipments.

In some cases, the evaluation of approval plans cannot be conducted in isolation from the consideration of other concurrent collection building methods, for one method frequently impinges on the others. Additional factors which may hinder the evaluator are time, lack of expertise, and incomplete records. There is a necessity for adequate planning, willing help, sufficient and reliable record keeping, and perhaps a cooperative vendor when approval plan evaluations are conducted. Even when these criteria are met, there may not always be a consensus on how the results are judged. But that is the nature of evaluations and perhaps why librarians are continuing to debate the advantages and disadvantages of approval programs.

## Notes

1. Jennifer S. Cargill and Brian Alley, *Practical Approval Plan Management* (Phoenix: Oryx, 1979).

2. Peter Spyers-Duran, ed., *Shaping Library Collections for the*

*1980s* (Phoenix: Oryx, 1980).

3. Association of Research Libraries, Office of Management Studies, *SPEC Kit 83, Approval Plans in ARL Libraries* (Washington: ARL, 1982).

4. Paul H. Mosher, "Waiting for Godot: Rating Approval Service Vendors," in Spyers-Duran, 159–166.

5. John H. Reidelbach and Gary M. Shirk, "Selecting an Approval Plan Vendor: A Step-by-Step Process," *Library Acquisitions: Practice and Theory* 7: 115–122 (1983).

6. Mary Lee DeVilbris, "The Approval-Built Collection in the Medium-Sized Academic Library." *College & Research Libraries* 36: 487--492 (November 1975).

7. Jan Gregor and Wendy Carol Fraser, "A University of Windsor Experience with an Approval Plan in Three Subjects and Three Vendors." *Canadian Library Journal* 38: 226--231 (August 1981).

8. Linda Ann Hulbert and David Stewart Curry, "Evaluation of an Approval Plan," *College & Research Libraries* 39: 485--491 (November 1978).

9. Edwin D. Posey, "The Approval Plan Experience of an Engineering Library" in Spyers-Duran, 110–114.

10. Anna H. Perrault, "A New Dimension in Approval Plan Service," *Library Acquisitions: Practice and Theory* 7: 35--40 (1983).

11. David R. McDonald, Margaret W. Maxfield, and Virginia G.F. Friesner, "Sequential Analysis: A Methodology for Monitoring Approval Plans," *College & Research Libraries* 40: 329--334 (July 1979).

12. Marion Wilden-Hart, "Long-Term Effects of Approval Plans," *Library Resources & Technical Services* 14: 400--406 (Summer 1970).

13. C. David Emery, "Efficiency and Effectiveness: Approval Plans from a Management Perspective," in Spyers-Duran, 1985–199.

14. Thomas W. Leonhardt, "An Approval Plan: How It Failed, How It Could Succeed: A Case Study in the Boise State University Library," in Spyers-Duran, 69--73.

15. Stanley P. Hodge and William Hepfer, "Selecting and Acquiring Scientific Materials for Academic and Research Libraries," in *Selection of Library Materials: Guides to Sources and Strategies* Particia McClung, ed. (Chicago: American Library Association, forthcoming).

# LIBRARIAN-FACULTY ROLE IN COLLECTION DEVELOPMENT WITH APPROVAL PROGRAMS

by

Sara Ramser Beck

## *Collection Development*

During periods of fiscal austerity in universities and colleges, it is imperative for librarians to be good stewards of university funds in general and collection development funds in particular.

Collection development funds are often eyed jealously as an undeserved largess by faculty members. Sound management practices and encouragement of active faculty participation in a well-conceived collection development program are essential tools in creating better understanding of collection development policies and promoting support for these policies.

To those entrusted with administering these funds, well planned collection development policies and faculty support represent enlightened self-interest as well as the fulfillment of professional obligations.

The library collection is among the most permanent and valuable assets of the university. Development and administration of judicious selection practices are the longest lived contributions a library director can make. The quality of the library collection is frequently an important factor in accreditation decisions by regional and professional accrediting agencies.

All librarians need to understand what the goals of quality collection development are and to share a sense of professional commitment to those goals. Efforts to create and sustain faculty members' understanding of collection development policies must be given high priority by the library administration. Faculty members need to know that the existence of an approval plan is one manifestation of modern management techniques of rational decision making and strategic planning of resource use.

A variety of techniques can be used to work toward these goals. An obvious approach would be to disseminate in-depth collection development information to faculty members of the library committee, if there is such a committee in existence. If the committee members represent a diversity of subject areas, the library committee could be a highly effective means of disseminating accurate information about collection development policies. Since it is usually the library director who meets with the committee, this approach would insure an interested audience receiving authoritative information. Committee members should be encouraged to share their knowledge with their faculty colleagues.

Involving all librarians in bibliographic activities and encouraging their active interaction with specific academic departments would be another way of increasing faculty understanding of collection development goals and policies. In order to be effective, mechanisms for insuring that librarians are knowledgeable in this area must be developed and maintained.

*Approval Plans*

The concept of approval plans is widespread throughout American libraries of all types and in college and university libraries in particular. It is reported that more than 80 percent of the libraries affiliated with universities and almost two-thirds of the libraries in smaller schools have, or have had, approval plans.[1] Despite their popularity, the purpose of approval plans is not always well understood on campus or even within the library.

It is often asked whether a better quality collection could not be built by selecting books on a title-by-title basis. After all, faculty members read reviews of new books in their discipline and are more than willing to make recommendations, are they not? The answer is both yes and no. Some faculty members take a very activist approach to keeping current on new publications in their disciplines; they not only read the reviews but are more than willing to recommend titles they want and need for their own scholarly research and the needs of their students. Other faculty members are less diligent in this area. However, books to cover the entire academic program of the university are required by students and scholars on all levels. The responsibility for policies to ensure collection quality lies with the library administration. This is the primary point to consider in formulating collection development policies.

Other factors of lesser importance to consider, in terms of relying on faculty requests as the major source for acquiring current imprints, are that many books of scholarly worth are never reviewed and that the reviews may not appear until sometime after the book has been published. Also, even faculty members who are conscientious in collection development activities may occasionally overlook reviews of books important to their discipline. However, faculty requests based on current book reviews are a vital part of the collection development program. These requests serve important functions. First, some requested books are not available via approval programs or would not be supplied because they lie outside the profile parameters. Second, these requests offer valuable feedback on the nature of the fit between the current profile and books being requested by the faculty. The requests provide a mechaism for data gathering regarding possible profile revisions.

Although the approval program alone is not sufficient for collection development of current imprints, it can be a valuable tool because initiating the program per se involves looking at collection development in a rational, organized way. Writing the profile (selection guidelines) of such an approval program involves pre-selecting subject areas in which books are to be collected, the depth of coverage, and the format of materials to be provided for each subject area.

This document forms the basis for a detailed collection development policy. Typically these decisions are made to serve the curriculum and research needs of the university community. The decisions made ahead of the time of actual expenditures can be made in a more reasoned way, reducing the effect of pressure by individual faculty members or departments.

The process of writing the profile should involve consultation with faculty members. Part of the acceptance of the end product is attained and facilitated by the decision-making process itself. Without the profile writing process, a library will rarely delineate its collection development policy so carefully or in such great detail. Encouraging faculty participation in decision making about books received via approval programs is one way of increasing faculty understanding and support of the collection development policies and the approval plans especially.

*Advantages*

The major benefit of an approval program is to acquire books in selected subject areas at the time of publication. To insure that the profile reflects current, not historical, curriculum and research needs, the profile should be given periodic reviews by subject bibliographers. Faculty advice in each discipline should be solicited if it has not been forthcoming throughout the year. The profile should be updated on a regular annual basis.

The most obvious benefits of approval programs are the following:

1. Pre-selecting titles on the basis of subject allows for rational decision-making with input from faculty members in all

subject areas, not just those with the most political clout.

2. Better quality of selection because the actual book can be examined. Faculty members can make recommendations from examination of the primary source not filtered through the opinions of the reviewers.

3. Increased ability to plan allocation of a significant portion of acquisitions funds and to purchase books at the time they usually cost least.

4. Reduced staffing requirements in acquisitions departments because the titles received do not require pre-order searching or in-house order preparation.

5. More predictable discounts from vendors.

6. Gaining optimum benefit from each title by having it available soon after publication.

7. Better service via well-established contacts with the approval vendor.

*Disadvantages*

The possible drawbacks to such an approval program are the following:

1. Books may be added to the collection without careful review to determine if the titles present relevant materials on a scholarly level.

2. Important titles may be overlooked for purchase if they are not supplied via the approval program.

3. Lack of involvement in collection development by faculty members and library staff subject specialists.

4. Lack of faculty and librarian awareness of new titles being added to the collection.

5. Not obtaining the optimum discount for each title purchased.

*Washington University*

Now let us examine how these theories about collection development are implemented at Washington University. Washington University is a cosmopolitan university situated just outside the city limits of St. Louis. Eighty percent of the student body comes from outside the metropolitan area. On-campus students come from more than seventy countries.[2] The university library system has almost two million volumes and is comprised of a central library and departmental libraries in each of the following disciplines:

Art and Architecture
Biology
Business
Chemistry
Earth and Planetary Science
East Asian Studies
Mathematics
Music
Physics
Social Work

Each departmental library is headed by a professional librarian who is a subject specialist. Washington University Libraries also have ARL membership.

*Washington University Approval Plans*

Currently Washington University has an extensive domestic approval program with Baker & Taylor and more specialized approval programs with Bertram Rota and Harrassowitz. More than $100,000 is spent on the domestic approval program during each fiscal year.

Washington University has a long association with approval plans as it was among the libraries to pioneer in the use of approval programs when the Richard Abel Company initiated this type of service to libraries. With the demise of the Abel Company, the programs of several vendors were examined and the Baker & Taylor Company was selected as the domestic approval vendor. We have had an approval program with Baker & Taylor for over a decade.

Washington University has carefully devised its collection development policy to secure the benefits of comprehensive approval programs while minimizing their disadvantages. The keystone of the policy is its emphasis on carefully monitored selection over comprehensive collection governed by the profile alone. Each title must receive affirmative action indicating that it is being selected for inclusion by a faculty member or librarian-bibliographer knowledgeable in the subject field. Books are not simply added by default.

Faculty members are actively urged to participate in the approval plan portion of collection development. Each academic department has an internally appointed faculty member who acts as the liaison person with the library. This liaison faculty member advises new faculty members in the department about library services, including the opportunity to examine approval books. Typically, this faculty member personally reviews each approval shipment.

Each professional librarian is offered the opportunity to become a bibliographer after being on the library staff for a year. Let me quickly point out that bibliographic duties are assumed in addition to the librarian's other job assignment. Even the Associate Director for Collection Development has the additional responsibility of heading the Public Services Division.

In so far as it is possible, librarians are designated bibliographers in areas in which they already have some subject expertise. Subject expertise is important but not the only aspect of bibliographic responsibilities. Bibliographers also serve as liaison to faculty members in their designated subject areas, and faculty book purchase requests may be sent to the bibliographers. Bibliographers often contact the liaison faculty members about the gamut of collection development activities. Bibliographers communicate frequently with faculty regarding purchases being considered.

When faculty purchase requests are for current imprints which may be received via the approval program, the Acquisitions staff routinely sends the requests to the appropriate bibliographer. This procedure helps in evaluating the approval program and noting possible needed revisions in the profile. Bibliographers have collection development responsibilities for their entire subject areas beyond the approval program. They seek faculty advice on new titles not supplied via the approval plan and may initiate orders for any book needed. Their advice is sought on replacement decisions; again the recommendation of faculty members may be sought in making the decision.

Another point of contact between bibliographers and faculty members is the microfiche database which Baker & Taylor provides. The database includes all titles selected for inclusion in the approval program. This fiche is replaced monthly. At this time the Baker & Taylor approval database is not institution-specific so knowledge of the profile within a subject area remains the responsibility of each bibliographer. Bibliographers are encouraged to check the fiche to determine whether a book or form for the requested title can be expected to arrive via the approval program. If the title is not listed, or if it was shipped more than several months ago, the bibliographer can request the title to be treated as a firm order.

*Procedures for Approval Books*

To increase and facilitate faculty participation, the approval program books are displayed in a secure room close to the public card catalog from Tuesday through Thursday on alternate weeks. During a book display week, acquisitions staff members put the books on display on Monday afternoon. Setting up a display of 400 books takes one staff member approximately two hours.

Books are sorted by LC classification designated by CIP cataloging. In the absence of CIP cataloging, the vendor's classification is used. Since no attempt is made to determine whether this will be the LC classification the library will use for cataloging, selectors often need to check more than one call number designation to cover their assigned subject area. Faculty members and librarians who are bibliographers may examine the approval books. Faculty members may examine books in any subject area of interest; however, they may recommend whether to select or reject books only in their own subject areas.[3]

Each Friday the week's book display is taken down. Acquisitions staff members sort the books into three major categories and several minor ones. The major categories are the following:

1. Books with CIP cataloging that have been selected for inclusion.

2. Books without CIP cataloging that have been selected.

3. Books that have been rejected.

Other categories include added volumes, serial volumes, books to be added to departmental libraries that catalog their own books, and problem books. Problem books are those that have been selected for more than one collection.

*Librarian Faculty Participation*

It sometimes happens that a single book may be selected by one reviewer and rejected by another. In such cases, the Associate Director for Collection Development serves as the arbiter. She may, and frequently does, consult faculty members and/or bibliographers. She also designates which collection a book should go to if it is selected for inclusion in more than one collection. A serious effort is made to use fiscal resources wisely by keeping duplicate titles to a minimum.

The Associate Director for Collection Development reviews all books that have been rejected and may change the recommendation. Faculty members and bibliographers may be consulted on any of these decisions. The books remaining in the rejected category are returned to the vendor for credit. Each book must have either a collection designation slip or a reject slip. If a decision has not been made when the display is taken down, an Acquisitions staff member inserts an unsigned reject slip. This will automatically place the title in the reject category which is reviewed by the Associate Director for Collection Development.

As an adjunct to the approval program, faculty members and bibliographers also review form selections which represent books selected for the vendor's approval program but outside the profile of the particular institution. These titles receive further attention only if selected; then the forms are searched and forms for books not already in the collection or on order are sent to the Associate Director for Collection Development for a decision on whether to order. She frequently consults with faculty members and other bibliographers in making her decision.

The regular and well publicized opportunities to examine approval books let the faculty know their opinions are welcome and indeed are viewed as an integral component of the collection development program. As you may suspect from your own experience, some faculty members frequently review approval books, some review them occasionally, and some never choose to participate in this aspect of collection development. However, the presence of the program is intended to encourage faculty involvement in collection development and to communicate on a continuing basis that books are not passively added to the collection without consideration of their worth.

Aside from the opportunity to examine new books in their subject areas, one of the participation incentives for faculty members is the opportunity to request rush cataloging for a title of particular interest. Another option offers the opportunity to be notified when the book is cataloged. This latter perk is not limited to titles selected in the faculty member's or librarian's own subject field.

Librarian bibliographers are expected to be actively involved in collection development activities and to participate in examining approval books on a regular basis. Their participation is noted because they sign selection or rejection slips for each book on display. Bibliographers are expected to notify their own supervisor or the Associate Director for Collection Development when they are unable to meet this professional obligation. The division head bibliographers (one for Sciences, Humanities and Social Sciences) or the Associate Director for Collection Development will personally review books in the absent bibliographer's subject area or will request another bibliographer to review books for that display period. In this way they have a real working knowledge of the approval program and the titles acquired through it.

A minor problem point is that some faculty members and bibliographers find it difficult to examine the display books on the designated days and express their desire for longer display periods. The current practice was developed to balance the need for adequate time for books on display to be examined and the need to keep the entrance to the display room constantly staffed so that books cannot be unofficially "borrowed" before they are clearly identified as library property or designated to be returned for credit.

*Program Improvements*

Through the Library Council which has at least one representative from each school of the University, a faculty member from each academic department who acts as a liaison between that department and the library, and librarian-bibliographers who also serve as liaison personnel in their subject areas, the libraries of Washington University seek to promote understanding of the collection development policies. Input for decision-making is decentralized to optimize involvement and commitment by faculty members and library staff. Nevertheless, continued fine tuning of the program is needed on an ongoing basis.

Within the current calendar year, the library plans to implement the following improvement goals for its approval program:

1. Monitor performance or profile to optimize use of available data.

2. Reduce the return rate to 10% from the current 12.8%.

3. Reduce additional selection of current imprints to 15% from the current 24%.

4. Query faculty to determine their suggestions for improvement.

5. Revise profile as indicated by data collected and analyzed.

6. Track materials initially rejected and then reordered to determine possible profile revisions.

*Conclusion*

Washington University Libraries find that the current approval programs and associated procedures allow for active faculty and bibliographer involvement in book selection, timely receipt of books as they are published, and optimal use of slim acquisitions staff resources. The Order Unit in Acquisitions consists of one professional librarian who has additional supervisory responsibilities plus three library technical assistants.

While planning enhancements to improve the system, we believe our present system allows us to be good stewards by making judicious use of university funds while we continue to seek faculty and librarian participation in developing a high quality collection.

Notes

1. Kathleen McCullough and others. *Approval Plans and Academic Libraries: An Interpretive Survey*. Phoenix: Oryx Press, 1977. p1.

2. *Bulletin of Washington University, College of Arts & Sciences, 1983–1985*. St. Louis: Washington University, p6.

3. See Appendixes A, B and C for sample forms.

Bibliography

*Academic Librarianship: Yesterday, Today and Tomorrow*. Edited by Robert Stueart. New York: Neal-Schuman, 1982.

*Academic Libraries by the Year 2000: Essays Honoring Jerrold Orne*. Edited by Herbert Poole. New York: Bowker, 1977.

*The Academic Library: Essays in Honor of Guy R. Lyle.* Edited by Evan Ira Farber and Ruth Walling. Metuchen, NJ: Scarecrow Press, 1974.

*Advances in Understanding Approval and Gathering Plans in Academic Libraries*. Edited by Peter Spyers-Duran and Daniel Gore. Kalamazoo: Western Michigan University, 1970.

*Economics of Approval Plans: Proceedings of the Third International Seminar on Approval and Gathering Plans in Large and Medium Size Academic Libraries*, West Palm Beach, FL, February 17–19, 1971. Edited by Peter Spyers-Duran and Daniel Gore. Westport, CT: Greenwood Press, 1972.

McCullough, Kathleen, Edwin D. Posey and Doyle C. Pickett. *Approval Plans and Academic Libraries: An Interpretive Survey.* Phoenix: Oryx Press, 1977.

*Shaping Library Collections for the 1980's.* Edited by Peter Spyers-Duran and Thomas Mann, Jr. Phoenix: Oryx Press, 1980.

# Appendix A

WASHINGTON UNIVERSITY LIBRARIES
COLLECTION FORM

PLEASE INITIAL AND DATE THE
DESIGNATED COLLECTION

GENERAL __________

AV __________

BIBLIOGRAPHY __________

REFERENCE __________

DESK __________
LATEST VOLUME IN REFERENCE
(EARLIER IN GENERAL) __________

LATEST EDITION ONLY KEPT __________

AV MIC __________

MIC PER __________

XXXXXXXXXXXXXXXXXXXXXXXXXXXXXXXXXXXX

ART __________

BIOLOGY __________

BUSINESS __________

CHEMISTRY __________

EARTH SCIENCE __________

MATH __________

MUSIC __________

PHYSICS __________

SOCIAL WORK __________

XXXXXXXXXXXXXXXXXXXXXXXXXXXXXXXXXXXX

SEND DIRECT TO:

EAST ASIAN LIBRARY __________

MUSIC __________

SPECIAL COLLECTIONS __________

URBAN STUDIES __________

VERTICAL FILE __________

FORM NO. 112
(REV. 3/82)

# Appendix B

BIBLIOGRAPHIC SEARCHING DEPARTMENT
WASHINGTON UNIVERSITY LIBRARIES

I recommend that this publication
be returned to the dealer for
the following reason(s):

(Please circle number)

1. Outside library collection policy
   a. reprint
   b. translation
   c. series or set other than volume 1
   d. type of publication excluded from profile
   e. language or publisher excluded from profile

2. Publication received on standing order

3. Has been/will be received from foreign source

4. Textbook: outside profile

5. Duplicate (Please note source of first copy)

______________________________

6. Library has adequate material on subject

7. Miscellaneous (Please state reason below)

______________________________

______________________________

______________________________

Recommended for return by:

______________________________
Initials Date

Approved by Principal Bibliographer:

______________________________
Initials Date

Form 313

PRIORITY

2

NAME:
DEPT:
PHONE:
BOX:

140B

PRIORITY

3a

ROUTINE
NOTIFY:

NAME:
DEPT.:
PHONE:
BOX:

140D

# EVALUATING AND SELECTING AN AUTOMATED ACQUISITION SYSTEM

by

Edna Laughrey
and
Mary Kay Murray

The decision to implement or enhance an automated library acquisitions system, while momentous in itself, is just the first step in what is likely to be a long, frustrating, but educational process. A myriad of further decisions lies ahead: whether to buy one of the more than twenty acquisitions systems already on the market and, if so, which one; whether to design and build your own customized system; whether to participate in an integrated system or to rely instead on modular packages; or, if you already have an automated system, whether to upgrade it with new enhancements. Each of these choices involves decisions based on the library's own procedures and policies.

How, then, do you move from the decision to do something to the point of selecting the right system for your needs? You need to be prepared to spend an adequate amount of time to review the functions you wish to automate and to carefully plan your search for the right system. If you have prepared with thoughtful analysis and investigation, you are almost sure to be satisfied with the result.

*The Decision to Automate*

No library should turn to automation because it is fashionable, or because its image will be enhanced, or even because it will save money. The selection of an automated system requires too great an investment of time and money to be taken lightly; great care must be taken to ensure that each step is the right one for your library at that time. You need to closely evaluate your reasons for automating acquisition functions. The motive for automation needs to be sound and involve objectives that are truly obtainable. Frustration and failure are all too apparent where the motive evaluation and very specific planning have not taken place. The reason behind the move to automate may be to resolve an existing problem or to prevent potential future ones. Whatever the motive, all objectives for automating need to be examined to verify that the automation will indeed fill the perceived need. Some of the realistic reasons for automating acquisitions functions are:

---- Improve control over funds

---- Contain or reduce costs

---- Prevent duplication of effort

---- Manage increased workload

---- Improve efficiency

---- Improve control of work functions

---- Provide multiple access to files

---- Utilize staff better

---- Utilize work space better

---- Provide more and varied reports

---- Provide more rapid service to users

---- Perform tasks in more timely fashion

---- Provide integrated system within library

---- Speed the generation of orders

---- Improve management information

An important consideration is whether your library can afford automation. Since acquisitions involves many repetitive routines and a variety of files which require space, it has always been a likely candidate for automation. As early as 1957, the University of Missouri Library was generating purchase orders on card-punch equipment, and in 1965 the University of Michigan Library developed a prototypic card-punch system which generated purchase orders, claims, cancellations, on-order files, in-process files, fund accounting, and sophisticated management reports. But libraries by nature tend to be conservative institutions, not the least because they rely so often on public funding, and this conservatism is reflected in the rate of use and acceptance of automated systems. Many libraries have just now reached the point at which it has become clear that automation makes sense especially in view of increased workloads and reduced staffing. To be sure, there are others so small, so marginally funded, or so uniquely situated that manual processing will continue to survive, but for most libraries it now appears they cannot afford *not* to automate.

The rapid development of computer technology in recent years means libraries now have a plethora of options. Some libraries are continuing to develop customized local systems like the prototypes at Missouri and Michigan, but many more are looking at systems developed by others. Networks and bibliographic utilities offer acquisitions applications; vendors of circulation systems have added acquisitions components to enhance their sales potential; several booksellers offer online ordering systems as a way to cut their own costs and increase their share of the market.

To one or another of these choices you will be entrusting not only a large, ongoing financial commitment but also the success or failure of your acquisitions program and, in a larger sense, your library's service to its users. You cannot afford an automated acquisitions system unless you can also afford to make a sizeable initial investment for planning, investigation, and screening. Anything else is a false economy.

*Initial Investigation Phase*

No automated system will succeed without institutional support. You may find it best to appoint a broad-based committee which will consider questions such as these:

---- Is there adequate administrative support?

---- Will ongoing funding be available?

---- Is there staff support?

---- Can administration, staff, and users reach a consensus on expectations?

---- Will the costs be worth the effort?

---- What will be saved – staff, time, space, money?

---- Will efficiency increase? In what sense?

---- Will service be enhanced? In what sense?

---- Will more management information be provided?

---- Will files be more accessible, to users as well as to staff?

Answers to these questions can be extrapolated from ad hoc internal studies, consultations with librarians at other institutions with acquisitions systems, the sizeable professional literature on automated acquisitions, and consultations with the library's various constituencies of staff and users.

The committee may find that some of those consulted are hostile for reasons based more on fear of the unknown that on reality. In such cases its mission should be educative as well as investigative. Where circumstances warrant, there is nothing wrong with a public relations campaign in favor of automation, but the committee should scrupulously avoid raising unjustified expectations. In no way should perfection be implied or promised, or the inevitable snags of implementation will bring resentments that could ruin the ongoing support essential to any system's success.

*Where to Begin*

Once your library has made the decision to automate, the first step is to appoint an individual as project director. While there is no hard and fast technical requirement, these qualities are essential:

---- Knowledge of acquisitions functions;

---- Understanding of systems capabilities;

---- Verbal and written communications skills;

--- Respect of staff;

---- Enthusiasm for the position.

This person's mission and authority to make decisions must clearly have the support of the library administration. It is also essential that he or she be released from all normal work assignments in view of the importance of the investigative process.

The project director will probably wish to appoint a task force to help with the investigation, but a team leader or project director is essential to coordinate it. Since the team's function is chiefly advisory, its members should be chosen for both their own areas of specialization and their enthusiasm for the task of selecting an automated system.

*Conceptualizing System Options*

The team's first goal is to evaluate the types of systems and determine if one is best suited to the library environment. This investigation should also help to determine if one type of system is totally unsuitable. The individual systems available within each type should not be questioned at this point. You need simply to determine if one type of system is the most or least practical for your environment.

*Locally Developed Systems*

In the early days of library automation, people thought of building a system as they would of designing a house: they had specific needs and wishes, and custom-designed something to fit them. Not surprisingly, these individualized structures are likely to be extremely expensive.

Many large institutions already have sizeable data processing operations which handle their informational needs. The library may wish to consider contracting for an acquisitions component which will interface with the large institutional "mainframe" facility. In such cases you should consider points like these:

---- Will reliance on the mainframe facility be any cheaper than going to an outside source? Sometimes, surprisingly, it is not.

---- Can you obtain access to other useful information in the institution-wide system?

---- Will this project receive a high priority from the data-processing staff?

---- Can you still participate in bibliographic networks?

In any case, whatever type of locally developed system you investigate, you must determine:

---- Does equipment available on-site meet system needs?

---- Is equipment maintenance guaranteed for an appropriate time span?

---- Are there equipment-sharing costs?

---- Are equipment costs within the project's budget?

---- Have equipment locations been determined?

---- Will the locations need air conditioning and other environmental provisions?

---- Will additional personnel resources such as consultants, systems analysts, programmers or library staff be required?

---- Can enhancements be added easily?

*Utilities and Modules*

You may wish to investigate the economics of standardization offered by proliferating bibliographic networks and utilities. Many of these are integrated systems with acquisitions components which interact with network cataloging modules, circulation systems, etc. In other cases, commercial sources offer modular acquisitions components which can be linked with whatever utility, if any, your library uses for its other activities.

*Technological Trends*

Bear in mind too that the potentialities of automated processing are growing constantly due to revolutionary developments in minicomputer technology, systems theory, and marketing. As marketplace competition increases and vendors gain experience with installations in a variety of operating environments, we can expect to see these trends continue:

---- Quantum increases in hardware capacity;

---- New systems functions;

---- Greater attention to user needs;

---- Interface with other bibliographic systems;

---- Competitive pricing.

This may well be an ideal time to be in the market for a system as long as the selection is based on quality as well as economy.

*Cost Structure*

Finally, you must choose from a variety of financial arrangements.

Some existing systems and packages can be bought outright, giving both the responsibility to maintain and the freedom to customize. Others are analogous to condominiums, which require both the purchase of ownership and the payment of a periodical maintenance fee; each customer's basic package is the same, but each customer is free to make any enhancements desired. The last option is to lease a system. Though the initial investment is less, customizing is largely proscribed and the system is yours only so long as you pay the "rent."

*Identifying Procedures to Automate*

Next the team should identify the procedures best suited for automation. Particularly likely candidates are the many repetitive routines which generate the files essential to an accountable acquisitions system. It is perhaps simplest to view these in terms of the desired result.

A. Up-to-date status records for library materials: Here you can provide system notification when individual items are under consideration, ordered, received, cataloged, claimed, cancelled, and paid for.

B. Current book-fund accounting: Automation can provide records for individual payments, status of individual funds and accounts, institution-wide financial status, and specialized financial reports.

C. External communications: This will include documentation for purchase orders, claims, cancellations, payment authorizations, and checks to vendors.

D. Internal communications: An automated system should be able to generate cataloging worksheets and reports for the library unit which requests each item.

E. Vendor performance studies.

F. Accession lists for library users.

Each individual library may well be able to add other procedures.

*Analysis of Needs*

Before you can begin screening different systems, you must develop a firm idea of what you are looking for.

*Preparing Your Specifications List*

You must determine what your irreducible criteria are in selecting an automated system. This is probably the most challenging part of the process, since you must ultimately distinguish your real needs from what might be called your "wish list."

Prepare a list of all the features you might seek in an acquisitions system, ruled with separate columns headed "Need," "Wish," "Length of File or Field," and "How to Purge." Then proceed through the list, marking the "Need" column for those things your system *must* do, and "Wish" for the features you would like the system to do but which are not absolutely essential. Then, where appropriate, note the file or field length you will need and specify how the elements should be purged.

Included here is a sample of one such list. As you will note, it is divided into sections, and each section allows the user to identify the need for the specific element described. While some items on this list may not be relevant to your library and other items you consider important may be missing, this sample provides a good basic listing to which you can add and subtract features as needed.

Once you have obtained the appropriate input from your various constituencies and filled out the columns, you have what amounts to your working specifications list for selecting a system. (Parenthetically, you need not consider these specifications final; once you actually begin considering particular systems, you may find you have changed your conception of what is essential and what is expendable.) Make multiple copies of your specifications list; you will use them later as checklists for evaluating automated acquisitions systems.

*Preparing Your Vendor Questionnaire*

Your next step is to prepare a list of questions which will help you evaluate the suitability of the systems you consider. A sample of one such questionnaire is included here. As you will note, it lists a number of questions dealing with the flexibility of the system in terms of the ordering function, fund accounting, serials check-in, interface issues, system capabilities and costs. Once you have revised this questionnaire to suit your particular needs, you should run off multiple copies, leaving room after each question for you to record

| *Order File* | "Need" In File | "Need" Searchable | "Need" Boolean | "Wish" In File | "Wish" Searchable | "Wish" Boolean | Size of File | How to Purge |
|---|---|---|---|---|---|---|---|---|
| Author | | | | | | | | |
| Title | | | | | | | | |
| Series | | | | | | | | |
| ISSN/ISBN | | | | | | | | |
| Imprint | | | | | | | | |
| Purchase Order Number | | | | | | | | |
| Former Purchase Order Number | | | | | | | | |
| Destination | | | | | | | | |
| Selector | | | | | | | | |
| Requestor Name and Address | | | | | | | | |
| Fund | | | | | | | | |
| List Price | | | | | | | | |
| Encumbered Price | | | | | | | | |
| Expended Amount | | | | | | | | |
| Payment Status | | | | | | | | |
| Order Date | | | | | | | | |
| Receive Date | | | | | | | | |
| Catalog Date | | | | | | | | |
| Claim Code | | | | | | | | |
| "Ship To" Location | | | | | | | | |
| "Bill To" Location | | | | | | | | |
| Vendor | | | | | | | | |
| Call Number | | | | | | | | |
| Acquisition Type | | | | | | | | |
| Material Format | | | | | | | | |
| Vendor Notes | | | | | | | | |
| Acquisitions Notes | | | | | | | | |
| Cataloging Notes | | | | | | | | |
| Material Status Notes | | | | | | | | |
| Language | | | | | | | | |
| Inputter Code | | | | | | | | |

| | "Need" | "Wish" | Length of File or Field | How to Purge |
|---|---|---|---|---|
| *Availability of Bibliographic Files* | | | | |
| Items on Order | | | | |
| Items Received and Not Cataloged | | | | |
| Items Cataloged | | | | |
| Items Awaiting a Selection Decision | | | | |
| Items Rejected in Selection Process | | | | |
| Items Cancelled | | | | |
| Other Bibliographic Database | | | | |
| *Serial Check-in File* | | | | |
| Series | | | | |
| ISSN | | | | |
| Imprint | | | | |
| Frequency | | | | |
| Claim Code | | | | |
| Vendor | | | | |
| Purchase Order Number | | | | |
| Fund | | | | |
| *Vendor File* | | | | |
| Name | | | | |
| Address – (order, pay) | | | | |
| Vendor Code | | | | |
| Special Instructions | | | | |
| Status | | | | |
| Date Added to File | | | | |
| Number of Open Orders | | | | |
| Number of Rec'd Orders | | | | |
| Amount Spent w/Vendor | | | | |
| Number of Orders Cancelled | | | | |
| Number of Orders Claimed | | | | |
| *Fund File* | | | | |
| Name | | | | |
| Code | | | | |
| University Acc't No. | | | | |
| Status | | | | |
| Purpose | | | | |
| Special Instructions | | | | |
| Date Added to File | | | | |

| | "Need" | "Wish" | Length of File or Field | How to Purge |
|---|---|---|---|---|
| *Destination File (Shelving Location)* | | | | |
| Name | | | | |
| Code | | | | |
| Address | | | | |
| Status | | | | |
| Date Added to File | | | | |
| *Selector File* | | | | |
| Name | | | | |
| Initials | | | | |
| Address | | | | |
| Status | | | | |
| Date Added to File | | | | |

the answers. The questionnaire will serve these purposes:

---- To help you further clarify your expectations;

--- To record vendor responses when you reach the interviewing stage.

Also, once you have decided which vendors to invite for demonstrations, you may want to send them a copy of the questionnaire so they can focus their presentations appropriately.

*Order System – Questionnaire*

Can orders be keyed from more than one terminal simultaneously?

Can an order be placed for multiple copies, multiple locations, and on multiple funds?

How long after order input is the order file updated?

Can we select the vendor?

How are orders transmitted to the vendor?

a. If print, is it a multiple-part form?

b. If online, is it only to a specific vendor? Do you know the inventory of the vendor?

Can the system produce lists by type of material, fund, vendor and selector?

Can we determine the data elements to be included in the list, including payment history for standing orders?

Is the claim automatic or on-demand? Do we specify a claim cycle for orders? Is that cycle adjustable after an order is placed? Is the cycle flexible enough to meet our needs?

Can orders be automatically cancelled after a certain time period? Who determines that time frame? Is the order automatically cancelled or must there be human review?

Does the order record reflect both receipt and payment?

How are records purged from the order file?

How are selectors notified that materials have been ordered?

Can the vendor reports be added to the system? Do they appear in the system instantaneously? Do they automatically adjust the claim and cancel cycle?

Can the system identify who input the record?

Can default values be set, and for which fields?

Is there enough file space to include all the information needed in each record?

Is there a vendor file?

a. How many vendors can we have?

b. Is a claim code associated with each vendor? Can we override the code for a specific order?

c. How is a vendor added? How is it changed or deleted?

d. Can we view the file on line? Is a hard-copy printout possible?

e. What statistics are available?

What search points are available?

Will the system accommodate multiple bill-to and ship-to locations?

Does the system support MARC format?

How many orders can be entered by one person in an hour?

Are the field lengths flexible?

What data elements can be changed on an existing record? How? What record is there of the original information?

How easy is it to correct data or errors?

How frequently can purchase orders be printed?

How are partial or short shipments handled?

Are cataloging worksheets generated?

Are statistics kept for the number of volumes placed, orders or volumes received, cancellations and claims?

Does the system automatically assign purchase order numbers? Can we override that assignment? Can we include a purchase order number from a previous system in the record?

Can received material be tracked through technical services?

*Fund Accounting – Questionnaire*

Are funds encumbered at the time of ordering? Is it instantaneous? Are we warned online if we overencumber?

Does the system allow us an adequate number of funds and accounts?

Can we prepare the type of reports we need for fund managers and administrators?

Do the reports allow us to keep a record of the budget? Adjustments to the budget? Carryover of deficit from previous year? Expenditures? Cash balance? Encumbrance? Free balance?

Are audit trails acceptable?

a. Can we trace the history of a specific order by fund and invoice?

b. How do we know when the check was written?

c. Does the system tell who processed the invoice and authorized the payment?

Does the system convert foreign currency? How?

Does the system pro-rate postage and handling charges?

How are taxes handled?

Can we make a partial payment? How is the encumbrance affected?

Does the system automatically total the amount billed on each invoice?

Are funds unencumbered and expended immediately after an invoice is posted?

Can the system handle two years of accounts? Can we post payments to either year?

Can invoices be processed on more than one terminal simultaneously?

Can invoices be paid without associating the payment with a record in the order system?

Can we record pro forma payments?

How are serial payments purged?

Can we change the fund so that we are expending on a fund which is different from the encumbering fund?

Will the system allow us to order and expend on multiple funds for one bibliographic item?

Can funds be added or deleted at any time?

How many payments can be associated with a record?

Do payments show in the order record?

How many payments can we make before posting?

Can claims for invoices be produced for material received but lacking invoicing?

*Serial Check-in – Questionnaire*

How many serials will the file accommodate?

What is the maximum number of issues that can be recorded?

Will the system alert us to claim missing issues?

Does it produce claims?

What is the maximum length of the serial title?

What acquisitions information is associated with the record?

Does the system allow for the anticipated receipt date?

Does it indicate the actual receipt date?

Can vendor notations be recorded?

Does the system indicate the call number for the material or give instructions on the routing of material?

Can lists of serial titles be produced? Is the payment history also listed?

*Interface – Questionnaire*

Does the system interface with other systems in our library or systems we plan to add?

Does the system interface with a bibliographic utility?

Does the system pass specific information on to other systems? What information?

Does the system receive specific information from other systems? What information?

Can the user profile information which will be passed from system to system?

What are the one-time costs associated with the interface? Continuing costs?

Can material be tape-loaded into the order or fund accounting functions? How? What data elements can be transferred?

*System Capabilities – Questionnaire*

How many terminals can be used simultaneously?

Can there be public access terminals? Is the display easy to understand? Can some files or information be restricted?

How many printers can be used?

a. What is the quality of the printed product?

b. What are the costs associated with the printer? Paper? Ribbon? Maintenance?

How secure is the system?

a. How does it prevent loss of data?

b. What backup is there to the system?

c. Is the system password-protected to prevent unauthorized access?

What error reports are generated? Do they contain enough information to help resolve the error?

What statistics does the system provide?

Does the system monitor vendor performance?

a. Number of orders outstanding with vendor? Received? Claimed? Cancelled?

b. Amount of money expended? Encumbered? Average discount?

c. Average number of days between order and receipt?

Which data elements and files are updated instantaneously? Which in a batch process?

What is the maximum system capacity for items such as orders, cancellations, payments per item, vendors and funds?

What humidity and temperature controls are needed?

What is the maximum distance advisable between terminal work stations? What distance can the terminals be from the computer or processor?

Does the system support a dial-in capacity?

What functions can be combined: order/receive, receive/pay? Must they be combined?

What management reports can be generated?

How frequently is the software revised? Will we receive the new version without additional costs? How much control do we have over software design?

How secure is the equipment? What special measures will we need to take?

What technical skills are needed to keep the system operational? What activities will need to be performed?

What quantity of work can be done on one terminal in one hour in terms of orders placed, materials received, invoices paid and serials checked in?

Is there a training function? What activities may be done in this function?

Can purchase orders be transmitted to the vendor through tapes and online?

Can vendor-produced information such as invoices, approval plan lists and status reports be loaded into the system? Is this accomplished online or through tapes?

*System Costs – Questionnaire*

What is the anticipated purchase price of a system? What are the price schedules? What is included and excluded in the price schedules?

What is the lease price per year? What is included and excluded?

What is the per use price? Are there minimum and maximum uses?

What costs are associated with site preparation and equipment installation and who pays?

Who pays telecommunication costs? What is included?

Who does software maintenance and at what costs?

Who trains the library staff and where?

a. How many people can be trained at once?

b. How long does training take?

c. What training aids and manuals are available? What quantity is available free? What costs are involved?

What are the ongoing costs for paper, ribbon, other?

*Identifying Possible Sources*

Now that you have a better sense of what a system should do for you, you can begin to locate possible systems vendors. This will, of course, depend on what your particular type of system is likely to be. If you are considering contracting with your institution's data processing facility for an acquisitions application, or if you wish to explore the acquisitions component of a network or bibliographic utility, your obvious first step would be to get in touch with the facility involved.

However, if you are considering a commercially developed system, you first need to know which products are on the market. No doubt you have already received promotional mailings, and perhaps personal visits, from vendor representatives. Other leads can come from reviewing professional literature regularly, attending professional conventions, and (not least) from contacting librarians at other institutions which have already impelemented automated acquisitions systems. Whenever possible, get references and performance evaluations from users; this will help you screen out some of the patently unsuitable vendors before you begin.

For each lead you develop, prepare a short report form. A sample report is included here. As you will note, it provides a brief data summary for each contact you will make.

*Report on Commercially Available Automated Acquisitions System*

| | |
|---|---|
| System Name: | Company: |
| Address: | Phone Number: |
| Individual Contacted: | Date: |

Customers where reference may be obtained (name of institution, contact person, address, phone number):

System available by purchase ______, lease ______, per use charge ______, other (specify) ______________________________.

| | |
|---|---|
| Description of hardware | |
| Installed in library: | Equipment (terminals, mini computer)<br>Number<br>Physical size of each |
| At host: | |
| Description of software | Program language:<br>Can library write or customize software? To what extent? |

Description of training guides and manuals:

*Initial Contacts and Screening*

Contact the market representative for each systems supplier on your list. Obtain and record answers to the items on the short report form; ask the representative to send brochures, manuals, etc., as well, when available. Comparing the information in these sources to your specifications list and questionnaire will probably allow you to screen out some unsuitable suppliers before you invest further time in them.

*Reference Checks*

For those who remain, contact all the customers cited as references. First determine if their institutional setting makes their experience relevant to your purposes; if so, ask them how they feel the system has met their needs. Ask for as much detail as they can provide, and record their answers while you talk. Given the selective nature of human perception, you may wish to talk to more than one person at the institution if possible; you may also wish to have more than one member of your team participate in the interview and record the data.

Naturally vendors will tell you only about their satisfied customers. If you should hear through the grapevine of a dissatisfied customer, be sure to contact that institution as well and record the details.

*Presentations*

By now you will have winnowed your original list down to a core of suppliers worth serious consideration. Given the size of the investment you will be asked to make, you are now entitled to a demonstration of the system's capabilities at your library.

Contact each representative to arrange a mutually convenient date for the presentation. Ask what facilities he or she will need: special electrical outlets, dedicated lines, audiovisual facilities, etc. You might well decide to forward a copy of your questionnaire so the representative can be sure to answer your questions comprehensively.

Now decide on the composition of the audience for the presentation. All the members of the team should be included, as well as representatives of the appropriate constituencies. Plan to provide all those who attend with copies of your specifications list and questionnaire so they can record the data as it is presented. Be sure as well to assign different team members with individual responsibility for the various sections of the documents so you can guarantee that each item is covered. In the interest of fairness, you should try to have the same group at each vendor presentation.

During the presentation take notes on every aspect; do not try to rely on memory. Ask questions freely whenever you find anything hard to understand. If you are receiving an online demonstration, be sure to notice if:

---- screens are easy to read

---- keyboard is easy to use

---- information presented is clear and logical

---- access to information is easy to understand

Once the presentation is over, convene your group to discuss their impressions of the system and record these too. Try to allow for human considerations as well. While you may find the first presentation impressive if only in its novelty, you are likely to downgrade your impressions of it with each subsequent vendor's presentation. Since careful attention to each presentation soon becomes wearing, you are also likely to grade later presentations more harshly because you are impatient to end the process. With adequate spacing between demonstrations and reliance on written records, though, you can minimize these natural tendencies.

*Selecting the System*

Finally you are ready to select the acquisitions system which best suits your needs. Once the demonstrations are over, you can compare notes on each system and no doubt eliminate a few more without too much difficulty. You will probably find yourself left with a few strong candidates, each of them strong (and weak) in different ways. Here you will probably have to review your specifications list once more, perhaps changing your mind again about what is essential and what is expendable. Ultimately, of course, you will decide on the trade-off you feel is best for your library and take the next step – the installation and implementation of the acquisitions system you have just chosen.

Each institution has unique policies and procedures for acquiring new systems. Some always require a bid process while others are satisfied if only one system is proven to meet the real institutional needs. The institutional requirements must be well-known to the project director and followed through each step of the selection process.

*Conclusion*

As I warned when I began, selecting the right acquisitions system is sure to be a long, frustrating, but educational process. With thoughtful planning, careful analysis, and painstaking investigation of the sort described here, it is sure to be a rewarding endeavor as well.

# COPING WITH LIBRARY NEEDS: THE APPROVAL VENDOR'S RESPONSE/RESPONSIBILITY

by

Dana L. Alessi

Approval plans marketed by vendors in 1984 differ markedly from their early predecessors of almost twenty years ago, although their outward trappings – and internal workings – preserve the intrinsic concepts first developed by Richard Abel.

During those halcyon days of the early 1960s, Abel observed that book budgets were growing faster than personnel budgets; a core group of publishers produced the majority of scholarly titles; these titles were often not on library shelves until eighteen months to two years after publication; and computerization held a key to efficient collection building.[1] From these observations, Richard Abel developed the approval plan, a method proposing more, faster, cheaper, and with fewer. In other words, libraries could acquire more materials from a core group of publishers with fewer people, cheaper processing costs, and faster than the traditional method of selection, pre-order searching and verification, order placement, and finally, receipt of the ordered item.

The computer was central to Abel's concept as it would be the mechanism to store the library's subject interests (i.e., the library profile) and to match the vendor's profiling of subjects and non-subject descriptors (i.e., levels, format, etc.) from the thesaurus with the library profile; from this match would be sent the final product – a book which could be either accepted or rejected by the library or a form which could be returned to the vendor for an order. By ordering books well in advance of publication and shipping at publication or shortly thereafter, the vendor could insure that most titles would be in the library before orders were generated; by the receipt of a pre-printed bibliographic form with the book, the library could eliminate the expense of pre-order searching and reduce the cost of order generation; by careful subject profiling, a library could eliminate titles not wanted for its collection.

Although many librarians enthusiastically embraced the idea of approval plans (the attractions of rapid collection building using state of the art technology while obviating the need for additional staff were enticing indeed), others were skeptical at best and vehemently hostile at worst.[2] That blanket orders, not that far removed from approval plans, had long been an established method of book acquisitions in American research libraries[3] mattered not one whit. Perhaps initial approval plan resistance developed as much from a fear of automation than opposition to the approval concept itself.

But because approval plans did seem to provide at least a modicum of efficiency for libraries, they flourished in spite of misunderstandings, apprehensions, and outright failures. The Abel bankruptcy in 1974 caused many libraries to reevaluate their approval plans and approval plan vendors, but it was clear that approval plans were here to stay as a method of collection development and book acquisitions.

If from 1964 to 1974 libraries adjusted to the approval plan concept, the period from 1974 to 1984 has seen a refinement of the various approval plans offered by vendors and an increasing number of libraries adopting either full-scale book approval plans or new title announcement services utilizing the vendor database. Smaller libraries, without budgets large enough to support book approval plans, have found the announcement services particularly beneficial.

Yet in spite of the twenty-year history of approval plans, in spite of the conferences discussing approval plans, the ever-increasing literature, the countless vendor visits and presentations to libraries throughout the country, in spite of the growing numbers of libraries with approval plans and announcement services, there is still surprisingly little understanding of the responsibilities the approval vendor and the approval library have to each other and how needs of libraries affect vendor decisions.

For a marriage to be successful, each partner must be willing to share, to give and take, to tolerate imperfections, and above all to communicate. Each partner brings a past history to the relationship, a past history which cannot be eradicated. Each partner naturally makes certain demands of the other based on assumptions. A successful relationship requires hard work from both parties; it rarely just "happens."

The approval vendor-library relationship is not unlike a marriage. Each brings a certain past to the relationship; neither vendors nor libraries are perfect; and it will take work to sustain a viable relationship. However, that relationship might be much smoother if both vendors and libraries accepted certain responsibilities regarding approval plans.

First of all, the vendor must take responsibility for selecting books wisely and well for the approval plan. Although it is recognized that approval plans cannot cover *all* new publications, particularly those from publishers allowing no discount or requiring prepayment, the approval vendor's buyers and publisher relations staff should constantly monitor review literature such as *Publishers' Weekly, Library Journal, New York Times Book Review*, and *Choice* to determine what publishers are worthy of treatment and to seek to obtain their inclusion on the approval plan. They should attend trade conventions such as American Booksellers' Association on a routine basis, not only for sleuthing out new publishers for inclusion on the plan but also to keep abreast of general publication trends. The approval plan vendor must be aware of his target market and attempt to obtain publications most likely to be of interest to that market.

Secondly, the vendor has a responsibility to profile a title accurately. The profilers should preferably be subject specialists in the areas profiled; if not, they should at least be generally knowledgeable about the subject.

There are two *caveats* about correct profiling, however. First, all approval plan vendors are at the mercy of publishers. It is not unusual for publishers to supply inadequate or misleading information, especially before publication. For example, a series title may be omitted from promotional materials – or even the book itself – as happened with a title which Blackwell North America recently treated. Fortunately a sharp-eyed library (which had had previous trouble with the series) caught the error. The library recognized the title as part of this particular series because of the color and design of the book jacket which serials staff remembered from their previous trials with this series. A call to the publisher resulted in, "We're sorry; we forgot to put the series title anywhere on the jacket or in the book; it was a simple oversight." Not such a simple oversight to the approval plan vendor who is trying to maintain the integrity of an approval plan and standing order database or to the libraries which blocked this particular series from the approval plan. There are countless other examples of publisher oversights – not indicating a book is heavily illustrated, or that it is not an original U.S. publication, or was originally published as a government document, etc.

The second *caveat* is that profiling a book is very much akin to cataloging. Just as two catalogers may classify a book differently and give it radically disparate subject headings, so too a profiler makes a descriptive judgment which may vary widely from a library's interpretation. Couple that with the pressure to process books through approval quickly (a profiler doesn't have time to consider, weigh, discuss, put aside, and consider again to make sure s/he is accurate) and it becomes clear that not all books may meet a library's subject judgment. However, there should be a substantial attempt made to give the title accurate and adequate subjects, non-subject parameters, and bibliographic description.[4]

Third, the approval plan vendor should ship on a timely basis.

Not only does this mean that the approval vendor should ship forms and books weekly but as close to publication date as is feasibly possible. However, what is timely shipping? All approval plan vendors have stories of libraries waiting for a title to arrive on the approval plan (it is always an *important* title – likely a best seller – or a book which a faculty member wrote). However, a librarian has perhaps seen the title at the local B. Dalton or Walden's (in the case of the best seller) or the faculty member and two of his closest, most influential friends have been into the library with book in hand. The approval vendor is then accused of slow service, even though he may have placed his order for that title several months before publication. Again, the approval vendor is at the mercy of the publisher. In the case of the best seller, the publisher may have shipped thousands of copies to bookstores in advance of publication date in order to have a better chance at being on the best-seller list at publication date and rising swiftly on the best-seller list after publication date. The vendor who needs only fifty copies will wait his turn and will receive the title only when the publisher decides to ship.

There will also always be "approval shorts." These result when either not enough copies are shipped from the publisher (publishers don't always read orders and instructions either) or the vendor has misprofiled during the preprofiling stage. At Blackwell North America, this most frequently happens when we suspect a title to be of U.K. origin and therefore to be treated by B.H. Blackwell, but it turns out to be U.S. origin. The vendor has no choice but to delay shipment to certain libraries and order the title, hoping that the publisher will supply quickly. Sometimes they do; sometimes they don't, always to the vendor's chagrin.

In short, the vendor has the responsibility to ship titles close to publication date, but there will sometimes be extenuating circumstances preventing timely shipping.

The vendor has a responsibility to provide management information to the library. This information may be of several types. It may be the number of books shipped for a given period, listed by author, title, or subject. It may be book returns for a given period as opposed to receipts; again, a subject order may prevail. There may be data regarding total expenditures by profile; average prices per book per subject, etc. For form selections, there may be data of the number of forms sent by subject and the number returned along with the corresponding dollar value.

The vendor has a responsibility to provide the library with reliable annual cost and coverage information by subject for all titles treated on the approval plan. These figures are useful for profiling purposes and increasingly helpful for budget allocation purposes.

The vendor must be honest – and honorable. McCullough took

vendors to task in 1972 for overzealous promotional literature.[5] Much of the literature promoting approval plans today (including sometimes some of our own, I fear) still makes overblown claims. In addition, the vendor has a responsibility to sell realities, not promises. All libraries have been victims of vendors, approval or otherwise, who make extravagant claims regarding discount, turnaround time, fulfillment rates, services, etc., and the expectation turns out far different from reality. To be sure, there are occasions when problems with service are beyond the vendor's control. The vendor *has* been accurate in selling services which do exist; but perhaps an employee in billing failed to follow correct instructions. If this happens, the vendor should not be excoriated for being dishonest in selling non-existent service. Beware of vendors promising the moon and stars unless they can back up their promises with references of those who have actually received the moon and stars; otherwise, you will probably receive just plain earth.

The approval plan vendor has a responsibility to clarify any policies a library may question. For example, when is a book *not* returnable? How soon must unwanted books be returned? Who is responsible for the loss of books before the library receives them? Who is responsible for the loss of books being returned to the vendor? The vendor should not be loath to state a policy, even if it is not a policy favorable to the library. The policy should preferably be stated in writing.

The vendor increasingly has a responsibility to let the library know what titles have been selected for the approval plan and what titles have been shipped, whether that information be in the form of a marked bibliography, microfiche, or machine-readable records in a database. A major criticism of approval plans was the uncertainty of knowing what had been selected and ordered for a vendor's approval plan. Some vendors had long been willing to mark the *American Book Publishing Record* or, in the case of U.K. imprints, the *British National Bibliography*. However, especially in the case of the *BNB*, titles were frequently listed either too far in advance of publication or too long after. In 1979 B.H. Blackwell, Ltd., was the first to create a reliable source, produced internally, for libraries to check to see if a given title was selected as a book, a form, a standing order, or was totally outside the library's profile. This tool, known as the *Blackwell's Book of the Week*, used the *BNB* as a backup to insure complete informational coverage regarding treatment of U.K. imprints and was shipped weekly with approval shipments. A monthly cumulative microfiche index provided access points to the *BBOW*. Following this successful attempt at taking the guesswork out of approval plans, Blackwell North America, Baker & Taylor and Ballen all developed their own microfiche listings. In addition, B&T utilized its automated acquisitions system, LIBRIS, to provide information to its approval libraries regarding selections.

Another vendor responsibility is to have a knowledgeable staff. The staff should be informed about the company they represent, its policies and procedures, the library world in general, academic librarianship in particular, and the publishing trade. The most knowledgeable should be those in everyday contact with the library – the sales representatives and library service personnel. Vendor management should take whatever steps necessary to insure such knowledgeability – attendance at professional meetings, participation in conferences, even the chance for operations staff to visit library operations.

Finally, the most important vendor responsibility is communication. This communication can take several forms – the periodic telephone call to find out if there are problems which can be solved before they grow into catastrophes; the letter which summarizes terms and understandings, especially at the start of a new approval plan; a written explanation of a profile; regular visits with acquisitions and collection development personnel; informal interaction at meetings; journals reviewing approval selections; and newsletters apprising librarians of new developments and enhancements to the approval plan. The problem of communication isn't new. It runs throughout library literature dealing with the library-vendor relationship. In 1956 David Busse, then Sales Manager of the Book Department at the now defunct A.C. McClurg Co. stated:

> "Communication provides our greatest problem. If the wholesaler were to know what the customer is thinking as he writes his order and *if the customer were to be more fully aware of what the wholesaler can do* [italics mine], I am certain that the customer would be served more efficiently and these problems would be solved."[6]

Not much has changed in almost thirty years. But the librarian can't be informed, even if s/he asks questions, unless the vendor assumes responsibility for communication.

But as a marriage is not a one-way street, neither is the vendor-librarian relationship. The library too must assume certain responsibilities if there is to be a good working partnership and a successful approval plan.

Although there is a fair amount of literature devoted to the library's responsibility to the firm order vendor,[7] there is very little concerning the library's responsibility to the approval plan vendor.[8] Yet the library does have many responsibilities which it must shoulder.

First, once the library has decided that it will embark upon an approval plan, there should be extensive preparation before the profiling session. Preparation includes identification of those staff members – professional or support – who will be involved in the vendor visit to profile and set up the appropriate internal arrangements – billing, shipping, etc. It includes examination of the vendor profiling information (often a thesaurus) to become familiar with structural organization, subjects, and non-subject parameters. If the profile is to be developed by subject bibliographers in consultation with faculty, it includes discussing what materials the faculty is particularly interested in receiving. The library must analyze how much money will be set aside for the approval plan and how it will be allocated – will books and forms be charged to one overall fund, will forms be charged against departmental allocations, etc. Current collection policies must be evaluated. Indeed, this advice sounds basic. However, many times the vendor will walk into a library to profile and it appears to be the first time a library has thought about the approval plan (although presumably there had to be some thought at some point or else the library would not be initiating such a plan). Having a curriculum catalog available for consulting during profiling is often very valuable but frequently not supplied. Yet preparation for profiling is one of the most crucial aspects in setting up a successful approval plan since it permits both the library and the vendor to understand at the outset of the plan basic premises and principles, organization, and parameters. Adequate preparation will often prevent problems after approval plan implementation.

In line with preparation, those most intimately involved with the approval plan will find themselves constantly required to educate other librarians and faculty about the approval plan. Education is a major responsibility of the library if it is to expect success on the approval plan. Education can take many forms – inviting the vendor to speak with librarians and faculty and explain the program. seminars sponsored by the library, one-to-one conversations, manuals describing the approval plan and the profile, handouts, etc. Because approval vendors are constantly changing and enhancing their product, and because there is always faculty and staff turnover, the education process is never-ending. One of the greatest satisfactions for a vendor is to walk into a library where the acquisitions or collection development librarian understands this responsibility and has taken the time to work through a profile carefully with a new librarian or has thoroughly explained the vendor's operational procedures to a new staff member.

The librarian has a responsibility to have basic publications knowledge, something everyone should have learned in library school but which is often lacking in too many librarians.[9] The librarian should understand publisher/distributor relationships, especially as these continue to increase. The librarian should understand the problems with delayed publications – that frequently a publisher will ship to bookstores first and only then to a vendor, or that publishers will announce a title for publication but postpone actual publication for up to two years. The librarian should understand the distinctions between series and serials and why certain serials cannot be supplied on approval. A vendor should not need to explain why *Books in Print* cannot be supplied on approval! The librarian should understand the nature of societal and association publications and why many of those are not appropriate – or available – for approval plan treatment. The librarian needs to understand how vendors acquire books for approval plans – and how publishers make their books available to approval plan dealers. (Even some *publishers* do not know how to make their books available!) The librarian should realize why certain publishers' books are non-returnable. Any good basic text on publishing or acquisitions should provide such knowledge.

Along with understanding the business of publishing, the librarian has a basic responsibility to understand the business of bookselling. Let us tackle the matter of discount first. "Libraries have asked for continually increasing discounts, and have taken advantage of sellers' competition to get them."[10] A quotation from recent library literature? Hardly. This quotation was taken from an article by Scott Adams which appeared in *Publishers' Weekly* in 1945. Mr. Adams also points out that scholarly books, traditionally given short print runs and low discounts, are at a disadvantage in a high volume, high discount trade book market. He also cogently states "If it costs [a vendor] 15% of his gross sales to do business and the best discount he can hope to secure from the publisher of a given technical book is 20%, and his library customer demands a 10% discount, he is out of pocket 5%."[11] Since 1945 the demand for discount has not changed, the discounts from publishers have changed very little (downward, if in any direction), but bookseller costs have increased. Bookselling is not a high profit business, for profits average 2–3% with 5% at best.[12] The bookseller, obviously, must make a profit to stay in business, but too many libraries, faced with their own budgetary pressures, fail to make allowances for this basic business fact.

Thus, even though a library might desire to receive many societal publications on approval, it should be obvious that an approval vendor, if he wishes to stay in business, cannot supply such titles, especially if the society in question requires prepayment, gives no discount, and does not accept returns.

As part of this basic responsibility to understand business practices, the library must accept a responsibility for prompt return of unwanted books and prompt payment. Publishers require booksellers to pay in thirty days. By the time a book is received by the vendor, profiled, matched to library profile, matched to library bibliographic slip, billed, shipped, checked in by the library, displayed, rechecked by library; by the time the invoice is approved for payment, often by three different offices, especially in state systems, and the check printed, mailed, received by the vendor and applied to the account, far more than thirty days have elapsed, during which time the vendor has paid for the book and is out the money. Because of the necessary internal vendor profiling and library display, approval titles take longer for payment than other materials. Efficient processing in the library can cut several days off the payment process.

A library must also realize that books should be returned promptly if not wanted. Most publishers set a time limit on the return of books from a vendor. Not every book a library returns will be placed back in the vendor's inventory; there are certain books, published by reputable presses, even university presses, which the vendor has a responsibility to treat on approval, but which, because of subject matter, author, treatment, etc., are rejected by libraries with such consistency that to return them to inventory would be foolhardy on the part of the vendor. But they can be returned to the publisher only if returned promptly by the library. Additionally, until a book is credited by the library returns department of the vendor, it will show outstanding on receivables.

Another corollary to understanding basic business practices is to realize that services cost money. The forms that come with the books cost for print stock, for computer time to run, for matching to a book. Management data cost paper, computer time, and postage. Changing profiles costs staff labor in input and keying, paper, computer time, and postage. The complimentary manuals and thesauri that vendors provide cost paper, staff time, postage. All vendors are willing to give these items as part of their service and understand that it is the cost of doing business. Realize also that form selections generated on non-book approval plans cost money to produce. It is only honorable that if a title is selected from the forms it be sent to the vendor who supplied the forms. As F. Seymour Smith in his article on librarianship and the book trade stated, "Trade should follow the service."[13]

The library has a responsibility to monitor the profile. If a rejection rate is high, the library should analyze why. Is it the overall profile causing problems? Are there budgetary reasons? Is a particular bibliographer or faculty member ordering too quickly and not allowing the approval plan to do its job? Is a particular bibliographer or faculty member rejecting titles which are then reordered? Are certain subjects no longer included in the curriculum but still included in the profile? Are there new courses added which the profile does not reflect? Are various non-subject parameters causing excessive rejections? Are there titles the library anticipated on the approval plan which did not arrive? The vendor can at best supply data regarding a high return rate; it is up to the library to interpret it locally. The vendor can supply the library a profile print-out; it is up to the library to determine if subjects are covered adequately. The vendor can supply a list of titles sent on the approval plan; it is the library's responsibility to note titles missed.

The library has a responsibility to provide specifics to the vendor if there are problems. It is not enough for a library to say "We're not getting enough coverage in biology." Specifically, what titles did the library expect to receive on approval which did not arrive? Could these logically have been expected to be sent? The vendor, supplied with specific titles for investigation, may be able to report back to the library that Title A was outside the price parameter set by the library, Title B was a publisher requiring prepayment, Title C a foreign title not distributed in the U.S., Title D profiled under a subject not included in the library profile. General impressions are not enough. If a library is dissatisfied with shipping procedures, what is wrong? Are boxes marked incorrectly, poorly packed, etc.? In what specific shipments did problems occur? Armed with specifics, the vendor can investigate the problem and report to the library.

Finally, ultimately, the library has the same principal responsibility to the vendor as the vendor does to the library – communication. This communication can take the form of letting a prospective approval plan vendor know the timetable for making a decision on an approval plan and letting unsuccessful approval plan vendors know the library's decision and reasons for it promptly. An unsuccessful vendor would prefer to hear the library's decision from the library itself rather than through the grapevine. Communication can take the form of asking questions regarding profiling, vendor procedures, or any kind of clarification the library needs. It can take the form of requests for statistics or reports or other data. Similarly, vendors are pleased to learn the results of studies a library may have prepared. Surprisingly, many libraries will not know a service exists from a vendor simply because they never asked. Although most vendors will try to keep librarians informed about services, they deal with many more librarians on a face-to-face basis than librarians deal with vendors. As a result, it is very easy to forget with whom what service was discussed. As has often been stated, there are no ignorant questions. A vendor will never think a librarian unintelligent if s/he asks even the simplest questions. We are more likely to think librarians unintelligent if they operate simply on assumptions or do not ask questions about matters not understood.

Assuming that both vendors and librarians accept and understand their basic responsibilities to each other, there can still be external needs and pressures which influence the success of an approval plan. Whether political or budgetary, whether caused by internal procedures or automation, these pressures force approval vendors and libraries to examine new methods of coping.

Frequently, the approval vendor must cope with political pressures the library faces. These pressures may come from faculty, librarians, or administration. Both the vendor and the librarians with whom s/he deals must learn how to adjust to these pressures.

Often, pressures will come from faculty and librarians, especially at the outset of a new approval plan.[14] In general faculty and librarians will have two basic concerns – the cost of an approval plan and its coverage. In libraries where faculty have traditionally controlled the purse strings and departmental allocations are zealously apportioned and guarded, an approval plan represents a real threat, as there are always fears that Department X may get more on the plan than Department Y and that autonomy over one's own funds will be diminished. How can a vendor alleviate fear over how much the approval plan will cost totally and by individual department? One method may be the cost estimate. Based upon a retrospective history for the past year (calendar, fiscal, or point at which the approval plan is to begin), it is possible to estimate by an entire approval profile as well as by each subprofile (which may correspond to campus departments, divisions, etc.) the number of books and forms anticipated and their dollar values. To be sure, discounts, return rates, and inflation must be factored in, but in general the library can receive a relatively accurate cost projection to determine if the amounts estimated fall within budgeting allocations. Indeed, the cost estimate was developed in response to continuing requests from librarians for a projection of the approval plan expenditures.

The second concern of faculty and librarians will be coverage. Expectations may differ from the realities of the approval plan. The persistent pressure from libraries to alleviate the concerns of whether or not a title would be treated on approval resulted, as we saw earlier, in the development of microfiche and hard copy tools to inform librarians and faculty alike of a vendor's treatment. Thus, vendors responded to library pressure and perceived needs. And, as we have discussed earlier, a librarian has the responsibility to educate faculty and other librarians about the approval plan through handouts, manuals, etc. But what happens if a librarian's best efforts fail and there are still nay-sayers? That is the time to call for vendor assistance. The vendor must be ready to assist in mollification of faculty and librarians. Often the vendor will say nothing a librarian has not said, but coming from the mouth of a "supposed authority," the words somehow make a difference.

And what of librarians who would scuttle an approval plan? Some librarians should be called rejection librarians rather than selection librarians. These are librarians who always have a very high rejection rate on an approval plan because a) they order many titles too far in advance; b) the titles they receive are always 1) not scholarly enough; 2) too esoteric; 3) not in their subject area; 4) not by a reputable author; 5) not from a reputable publisher; 6) too expensive. After reviews of their rejected items appear, however, they invariably reorder. When asked why they do not like the approval plan, they will inevitably tell the collection development and acquisitions librarians that it is because the vendor does not cover enough material. In this case, it is up to the vendor to provide the flexibility of profiling by level, treatment, subject, publisher, and price to satisfy that librarian, even if it means seemingly endless revisions of the profile.

A second pressure on the approval vendor and library may be budgetary. In most cases of recent years, budgetary pressure has been caused by a shortage of funds; in some recent instances, it has been caused by an excess of funds.

The development of the cost estimate capability is one method vendors have used to predict expenditures. However, in recent years, libraries, especially those in state institutions, have found themselves having to take percentage decreases in the materials budget in the middle of a fiscal year. While the cost estimate can be used after cuts to insure that the library has cut enough, it does not offer much assistance to either library or vendor facing other problems which budget cuts generate.

The most common method of cutting a profile is to set the entire profile back to forms. This will eliminate many of the advantages of an approval plan (timely receipt, searching, etc.) and tends to create an uneven collection. It also puts extraordinary pressures on the vendor. The primary problem for the vendor is that the vendor may have ordered titles several months ahead, anticipating shipping them on approval. By the time the books arrive, several libraries may now have their profiles set at Form; thus the books become excess inventory. A second problem is the flip side of too much inventory. The vendor may be in the process of a major seasonal buy. The determination of how many copies to buy is done by a preliminary match against profiles. If many libraries have approval books programs turned off to forms, the buy will be skewed. Thus, the vendor must anticipate library budget cuts.

Happily, many libraries, with vendor assistance, are looking at other methods of cutting approval plans. These methods can include cutting back to U.S. origin only, lowering upper price limits drastically, raising lower price limits, accepting only unnumbered series, putting stringent geographic subject coverage limitations into force, increasing returns, cutting back to university presses only, and, as a last resort, evaluating subject coverage, especially if subject coverage has been unsatisfactory. However, the constant cuts and revisions, which must always be done quickly, put pressures upon the vendor to be efficient and prompt in processing library requests.

A third reaction to budgetary problems and approval plans is one forecast by H. William Axford in 1979. He said:

> "I also suspect that [the political implications of higher education's funding prospects . . . and our rapidly developing capabilities for cooperative collection development and effective resource sharing] will affect standing orders . . . resulting in the elimination of the operational problems caused by titles in series. By this I mean that libraries which have an approval plan will probably adopt a policy of acquiring only those titles in series that match the institutional profile."[15]

Mr. Axford has proved prescient. Increasingly libraries are cancelling long-held standing orders which tie up valuable monies, in order to let such titles rise and fall on their own merits in the approval plan and to be selected on a title by title basis. This trend, while certainly logical for libraries, has placed pressures on vendors to react. As vendors, we must be doubly careful that we profile a series title correctly and give it the proper series information. We at B/NA have also reacted to this pressure by increasing a library's options for action on a series title. In some cases, a library has a choice of six different actions it can take regarding a series title. Complex? Yes, but it is developed from libraries' handling of series titles in many different ways – e.g., separate departments; not setting up standing orders at all; setting up only limited standing orders, etc.

A fourth method of vendor coping with library budgetary problems has been the deposit account. Both firm order and approval vendors have set up formalized mechanisms whereby a library can deposit a significant amount of money and receive either credited interest or additional discount. Not only does the deposit account provide additional funds to the library for purchase, but it also protects library money which may be vulnerable to loss at the end of a fiscal year or even during the fiscal year in the case of expenditure cutbacks.

All approval vendors and many libraries have become experts at cutting approval plans and using the vendor's thesauri to accomplish that purpose. However, in the last few years a phenomenon rarely seen since the 1960s has arisen – a library suddenly receives a substantial appropriation, often well over $100,000, to purchase retrospective materials or to build the library collection.

In days past, a library often expended its newly found riches for retrospective purchase on desiderata it had accumulated over the years, on large microform sets, on backruns of journals, or even on the purchase of entire libraries or bookstores. But desiderata were often out-of-print and unavailable before expenditures had to be completed, large microform sets were generally unused, backruns of journals were not always available, and library and bookstore collections were not always wisely chosen and had a high rate of duplication.

But the approval plan vendor had a ready tool for retrospective collection building – the approval plan database. Since the database was relatively current, the majority of titles could be expected to be still easily obtainable from publishers or, if out-of-print, from out-of-print sources. Because approval plan vendors concentrate on academic libraries, the scope of the materials was automatically appropriate. Because of the subject thesaurus approach, a library could develop only those subjects in which the collection needed strengthening. Because of the computer-generated forms, the library could save substantial order processing time.

A paper given by Pamela S. Cenzer at the Fourth International Conference on Approval Plans and Collection Development in Milwaukee in1979 is the only article in the approval literature which describes the use of an approval plan database in collection building.[16] In this paper, Ms. Cenzer describes the process whereby in 1977 the University of Florida used the Blackwell North America database for a retrospective collection development project for 1972--1976 imprints. This paper is essential reading for anyone contemplating a large scale retrospective collection building project. However, for the Florida project each and every one of the titles selected out of the 55,000 forms generated had to be searched against the card catalog to guarantee non-duplication. Shortly after the publication of this paper, Calvin Boyer, then Director at the University of Mississippi Library, approached B/NA with the suggestion that since B/NA's records were in a modified MARC format (B/NA MARC), and that since many libraries using OCLC for cataloging also had machine readable records in MARC format, that it might be possible to match the two records using LC card number and ISBN number. While all duplicates might not be eliminated, at least a significant portion would be. Dr. Boyer originally broached the suggestion for a retrospective project the University of Mississippi was anticipating.

That particular project never came to fruition, but about one and a half years afterward, B/NA was approached by Trinity University, San Antonio, Texas, to do a similar collection project. In Trinity's case, B/NA matched Trinity's approval profile to B/NA approval records from 1970 to 1979. The tape containing these records was sent to Trinity where, with the general assistance of MARCIVE, a 3 x 5 card was produced with pertinent bibliogrpahic and subject information after the B/NA records had been matched against Trinity's own machine readable records of its holdings. From the cards which were selected for purchase, Trinity then generated an OCR label containing B/NA's unique book number and the first three key words of the title. These labels were sent to B/NA for keying into the B/NA database, whereupon the computer-produced forms to accompany the book were generated and the titles ordered. The entire process saved Trinity a great amount of labor; an estimated 97% of all duplication was omitted. The approval database tape match is now an accepted method for large retrospective runs. Had not the need been there from the library, such a capability might have gone unnoticed.

Finally, approval plan vendors face pressures from developing library automation. One pressure – and easiest to deal with – has come from libraries which are beginning to collect in areas outside the traditional book – specifically software. It has been easy enough to begin to add software packages from major publishers to approval plans, although there can be several problems with working software into the regular bookstream and profiling. For example, a software package may be written for four different computers. Does the approval vendor then generate four forms – one for each package? At present there is no method of identifying by computer type for profiling. There are also questions regarding returnability problems, discounts, and supply. No doubt as more software is published, profiling sophistication will increase and new, specific, software nonsubject parameters will be developed. As with many enhancements to approval plans, it will probably be the customers who will offer valuable suggestions for software treatments.

Of more interest – and causing greater problems – are the pressures created by various acquisitions systems and the desire of acquisitions librarians that systems interface. Vendors have long been able to supply approval records and invoicing on tape – witness the BATAB system of years ago. An article written by Godden and Newborn in 1980 details Howard University's experience with B/NA's MARC records.[17] The results of their experience indicated that they were able to save money and time in processing and payment in addition to achieving increased accuracy. It should be noted that Howard had a local in-process control system. Baker & Taylor's

LIBRIS has provided a vendor approach to online access to approval records.

But acquisitions librarians are interested in how machine readable approval records can interface with other systems which are neither jobber-oriented nor local. A major test is now taking place at California State University–Long Beach, which utilizes the Innovative Interfaces acquisitions system. The goal is for approval records for individual libraries to be transmitted by vendors through the acquisitions system to the libraries themselves. Additionally, the BOOKLINE system promises to have the same capability, and it is to be expected that other systems will rush to develop similar capabilities.

Other libraries are investigating the receipt of machine readable records for selection purposes. For example, George Washington University Medical Library currently receives announcements of titles matching their profile in tape format rather than on bibliographic forms. The tape is input into their database; for titles selected, an order is generated and the open order immediately transferred to the database.

Through the MARC format, through ISBN's, through the BISAC format, it is clear that libraries will increasingly expect machine readable records which can be input into individual systems; in time, as the George Washington experience indicates, machine selection will not be uncommon. These are new pressures for vendors to deal with, pressures which will not have simple or inexpensive solutions.

From the days of the 1960s, approval plans have grown and matured. We can anticipate that in the next twenty years we will see startling changes in the operations of approval plans – online editing, online selection, interfaces with systems. Will every library have an approval plan? No. Will there still be those scoffers at approval plans? Probably. Will acquisitions librarians and vendors understand their responsibilities to each other? Hopefully. Will approval plans still exist? Most definitely.

## Notes

1. H. William Axford, "Approval Plans: An Historical Overview and an Assessment of Future Value," in *Shaping Library Collections for the 1980's*, eds. Peter Spyers-Duran and Thomas Mann, Jr. (Phoenix: Oryx Press, 1980) pp. 20–21.

2. For an excellent bibliography of early reactions to approval plans, see Kathleen McCullough, "Approval Plans: Vendor Responsibility and Library Research: A Literature Survey and Discussion," *College and Research Libraries* 33 (1972): 368–84. Also of value are the papers in Peter Spyers-Duran and Daniel

Gore, eds. *Approval and Gathering Plans in Academic Libraries*. (Kalamazoo, MI: Western Michigan University, 1970).

3. Robert Vosper, "The Blanket Order: Some Historical Footnotes and Conjectures" in Spyers-Duran and Mann, *Shaping Library Collections*, pp. 4--17, and Robert Wedgeworth, "Foreign Blanket Orders: Precedent and Practice" *Library Resources and Technical Services* 14 (1970): 258--68 are interesting reading regarding the development of the blanket order.

4. CIP data has been most useful for profiling assistance.

5. McCullough, "Approval Plans," pp. 375--76.

6. David Busse, "The Role of the Wholesaler," in University of Illinois Library School. *The Nature and Development of the Library Collection*. (Champaign: University of Illinois, 1957) pp. 104--116.

7. For a good discussion of this topic see Dimity Berkner, "Communication between Vendors and Librarians; the Bookseller's Point of View," *Library Acquisitions: Practice and Theory* 1 (1979): 85--90. See also James C. Thompson, "Booksellers and the Acquisition Librarian: A Two-Way Relationship," *Library Acquisitions: Practice and Theory* 1 (1977): 187--91.

8. Some papers in *Shaping Library Collections* cursorily deal with this topic, notably Robert C. Miller, "Approval Plans: Fifteen Years of Frustration and Fruition," pp. 43--53 and Milton T. Wolf, "Approval Plans: A Paradigm of Library Economics" pp. 178–84.

9. I am indebted to Donald Grant Stave, Approval Plan Coordinator at Blackwell North America, for his advice concerning this segment of the paper. For Mr. Stave's own attempt to educate librarians about the internal workings of an approval plan, see "Approval Book Acquisitions: Some Vendor Requirements and Practices," *Shaping Library Collections*, pp. 135--42.

10. Scott Adams, "Libraries and the Book Trade: Three Suggestions," *Publishers' Weekly* 147 (1945): 2360–63.

11. Ibid., p. 2360.

12. Michael Markwith, "Turning and Turning in the Widening Gyre:

Some Thoughts on the Publisher-Bookseller Relationship," *Library Acquisitions: Practice and Theory* 2 (1978): 30, and Thompson, "Booksellers and the Acquisitions Librarian," p. 190.

13. F. Seymour Smith, "Librarianship and the Book Trade" in Robert L. Collison, ed. *Progress in Library Science 1966* (Hamden, CT: Shoestring, 1967), p. 4.

14. Many of these pressures are also applied by librarians.

15. Axford, "Approval Plans," p. 26.

16. Pamela S. Cenzer, "Retrospective Buying Using an Approval Plan Database" in *Shaping Library Collections*, pp. 79--83.

17. Dennis E. Newborn and Irene P. Godden, "Improving Approval Plan Performance: A Case Study" *Library Acquisitions: Practice and Theory* 4 (1980): 145--55.

Bibliography

Adams, Scott. "Libraries and the Book Trade; Three Suggestions." *Publisher's Weekly* 147 (1945): 2360–63.

Axford, H. William. "The Economics of a Domestic Approval Plan." *College and Research Libraries* 32 (1971): 368--73.

Berkner, Dimity. "Communication between Vendors and Librarians; the Bookseller's Point of View." *Library Acquisitions: Practice and Theory* 3 (1979): 85--90.

Busse, David. "The Role of the Wholesaler." In *The Nature and Development of the Library Collection*. Champaign: University of Illinois Library School, 1957.

McCullough, Kathleen. "Approval Plans: Vendor Responsibility and Research: A Literature Survey and Discussion." *College and Research Libraries* 33 (1972): 368–381.

Markwith, Michael. "Turning and Turning in the Widening Gyre: Some Thoughts on the Publisher-Bookseller Relationship." *Library Acquisitions: Practice and Theory* 2 (1978): 29--32.

Newborn, Dennis E. and Godden, Irene P. "Improving Approval Plan Performance: A Case Study." *Library Acquisitions: Practice and Theory* 4 (1980): 145--55.

Smith, F. Seymour. "Librarianship and the Book Trade." In *Progress in Library Science 1966*, edited by Robert L. Collison. Hamden, CT: Shoestring, 1967.

Spyers-Duran, Peter and Daniel Gore, eds. *Approval and Gathering Plans in Academic Libraries*. Kalamazoo: Western Michigan University, 1970.

Spyers-Duran, Peter and Thomas Mann, Jr., eds. *Shaping Library Collections for the 1980's*. Phoenix: Oryx Press, 1980.

Thompson, James C. "Booksellers and the Acquisitions Librarian: A Two-Way Relationship." *Library Acquisitions: Practice and Theory* 1 (1977): 187--91.

Wedgeworth, Robert. "Foreign Blanket Orders: Precedent and Practice." *Library Resources and Technical Services* 14 (1970): 258--68.

# THE APPROVAL PLAN – THE CORE OF AN ACADEMIC WHOLESALER'S BUSINESS

by

Gloria Frye
and
Marcia Romanansky

Almost twenty years have elapsed since approval plans, as known today, were first established in academic and research libraries. Since that beginning many vendors, recognizing needs, evaluating customer demands, and surveying prospective customer expectations, have added approval plans as the premier service for university and research libraries.

From the vendor's perspective, an approval plan is not just a strategy to sell books but a professionally operated service technically designed to provide titles as quickly and efficiently as possible to libraries that desire to approve books before adding them to their collections.

An approval plan is not a reviewing tool but a collection development device that enhances a library's other selection procedures. It is not a plan or service that is rigidly standardized in all aspects; it is a customized service that reflects the specific and special needs of individual libraries. The vendor sees it not as the answer to *all* collection development needs but as a service that can meet *75%* or more of a library's requirements for scholarly, academic titles.

After defining the concept within its own organization, the vendor had to analyze the benefits of such a service for the company as a whole. The first benefit perceived was the opportunity to expand the current database. If a vendor planned to offer this service to an elite group of libraries, it had to provide as many publications as possible from as many publishers as possible. A vendor who supplied academic and research libraries through its firm order service had already developed an extensive database based on title-by-title ordering. However, with an approval plan, the vendor had to go beyond what the libraries were already ordering, beyond the bibliographic mainstream, so to speak. The vendor would have to identify virtually every title suited to the academic marketplace. "Identify" is the key word here. Since each library has different collection needs, suitability of titles must be left to the discretion of the approval plan users. Therefore, the vendor had to search out these publishers, such as societies, associations, and university affiliates, who did not actively promote their publications. Small commercial and university presses also had to be queried. The vendor saw its mission as supplying academic publications from all publishers that would supply a wholesaler. Thus, database expansion meant that the vendor could better supply all academic and research libraries, thereby further expanding business in this marketplace.

More publisher contact and greater quantity purchases mean that the vendor can negotiate for better discounts. Improvement of the discount system allows the vendor to pass on savings to the libraries. The vendor then has the opportunity to increase its business to a larger number of libraries – libraries that are concerned not only about receiving titles quickly and efficiently but also about the costs of publications.

More publisher contact also means that the vendor has to have more qualified staff – people who are knowledgeable about the publishing world. Qualified people in an organization means, of course, innovative thinking and planning, resulting in better services. Increased contact and high volume purchasing mean greater clout with publishers. Consequently, the vendor receives more attention from these publishers which means quicker response, thus improving fulfillment.

Searching out new publishers is an important part of the title file expansion process. By the use of approval plan audits, CIP, MARC, *Publishers Weekly, Choice*, etc., the vendor has the opportunity to discover new publishers, thus honoring its commitment to provide comprehensive coverage. In expanding its database to accommodate approval plan users, the vendor has the opportunity to improve its standards for bibliographic control. By its very nature, an approval plan forces a vendor to be as professional in its bibliographic data control as it is businesslike in its operations. The approval plan is designed to provide monographs as efficiently as possible. Part of this efficiency consists of providing data that accurately describes the book so that librarians can determine clearly the elements necessary for processing the title. By adhering to a recognized bibliographic code, the vendor makes it possible for the library to link new approval plan books to others already in the collection through author, series statement, edition statement, etc.

The interfacing of the approval plan with other services, such as standing orders, firm orders, and online acquisitions systems, is another important benefit to the vendor. The interface supports the consolidation of the acquisitions functions, thereby allowing the library to operate an approval plan with minimal changes in established procedures. Thus, the vendor has a strong selling point as well as a service that can produce more business.

The interface of standing orders and firm order services with the approval plan not only reduces unintentional duplication but, from the vendor's perspective, allows the two services to complement each other by further expanding the databases and by placing the services in a position to be known and desired by academic and research libraries. This allows the vendor to increase market share. The interface becomes a marketplace strategy for the multi-service vendor. Reduction of unintentional duplication results from the interface of services. Without such an interface, firm orders and standing orders would invariably cause excessive duplication. This reduction benefits both the library *and* the vendor by keeping returns low. Handling and shipping costs are reduced at both ends.

The ability to interface with the technology of other vendors is increased based on the size of the vendor's installed customer base. When a vendor has many approval plan customers, interfaces with various support services such as online cataloging and circulation systems become profitable for those designing and selling the interfaces. The larger the actual and potential customer base, the more interest in the commercial interface.

All these benefits are highly visible to libraries whether they are approval plan users or not. Less obvious benefits that also accrue indirectly to libraries result from improved inventory management and an understanding of the life cycle of the book. It is the goal of any vendor to turn inventory as quickly as possible. The advantages are obvious: it provides cash flow; it reduces expenses for interest on borrowed capital; and it increases profits. As a vendor acquires more customers, it is able to turn its inventory many more times. Thus, one attraction of an approval plan is that it increases the vendor's opportunity for profitable inventory turn.

At the same time inventory is being managed, the vendor is conscious that each book is a separate product and has a distinct product life cycle. The total life cycle of the book is dependent upon many factors, and no two books, even two published in the same month, on the very same day, have a product life cycle that is exactly the same. Consider the life cycle as it relates to a book. In the first stage, the Market Introduction stage, a new product is being introduced to the market. Most customers are unaware of that product. In the case of a book, the first libraries to receive the new title are those that have approval plans or standing orders.

In marketing terms, those who buy the product early in the product life cycle are called "early adopters of the product." Since print runs are short for many titles due to the cost of capital and cash flow problems in the industry, these early adopters will consume a large portion of the available copies. The library without such gathering strategies is at risk because available inventory may be exhausted before the second stage even begins. For many titles, order decisions will be delayed until the second phase of the product life cycle – Market Growth. During this period, there is advertising in the library-oriented journals, *Choice, Library Journal, Publishers Weekly* and *New York Times Book Review*, and sales rise. Later in this stage, reviews praising the book appear and also boost sales.

The next phase is called Market Maturity. Sales will generally be down from the previous stage. Competitors will introduce similar titles that have a much shorter life cycle but still provide a great deal of competition to the original product at this stage. The final period is called Sales Decline, produced by market saturation and diminished interest. Sales dwindle.

The total life cycle of a book may be as short as ninety (90) days or it may span years. Some titles by nature have shorter life cycles. In the case of annuals, such as *Ulrich's*, the life cycle is designed to be a mere six (6) months. The inclusion of a title in an approval plan will definitely affect its life cycle. The approval plan provides the book with exposure to its marketplace earlier in the cycle. Sales for the title will therefore peak earlier. Circulation of the title in the library will be higher since availability has coincided more perfectly with the demand created by the heavy advertising and promotion traditional in the first stage of the life cycle.

The acquisitions librarian is a key participant in the purchasing function and, like a purchasing agent, wants to ensure that the arrival of the book does coincide with demand. It is even better to have the book arrive before demand peaks. Should it arrive after the demand, the patrons will view this as a failure of the library's purchasing organization. In the case of important titles, especially those with high visibility, the librarian would like to acquire them as early as possible in the life cycle. Early acquisition of these books is accomplished through an approval plan.

As the manager of the purchasing function, the acquisitions librarian is concerned with all the aspects of the library-vendor relationship. As in any institutional buying situation, the reliability of the vendor in delivering the products, the final price paid, and the level of customer service provided are key factors influencing the future of this relationship. Since an approval plan is at the core of the library's acquisitions program, the dynamics of this relationship become even more important.

Keeping in mind the life cycle of a book, one can understand the vendor's need for accurate advance buying information. Not only does the approval plan provide the vendor with the opportunity to sell consistently in a given subject area, it also provides the opportunity to predict sales of the same titles in the direct order business. Since approval plan users are the libraries in the forefront of collection development, their buying patterns are useful guides for the vendor. With a precise indication of inventory requirements, the vendor is able to buy close to actual need, thus eliminating costly returns to publishers.

In addition to good inventory management, the vendor must also meet the high customer service requirements of approval plan users. Customer expectations are high. First, the library has committed a major part of its resources to a comprehensive method of gathering books. Since the success of the library purchasing activities depends a great deal on the success of the approval plan, the library needs to ensure that each of the services promised by the vendor is delivered. For example, failure to modify a profile to correspond to curriculum changes may result in a lack of books for a new area. The vendor's inability to supply books outside the profile and invoice to the approval plan when directed to do so by the library may result in excess funds remaining in the approval account.

Second, the library may have chosen a particular vendor for the services promised and may have traded discount points for these service features. The librarian must therefore monitor the services actually provided by the vendor.

Third, the library perceives itself as a member of an elite group of users. It naturally follows that the vendor's services should be on the same level with the needs of this elite group. The vendor is dealing with very experienced librarians engaged in the purchasing function. They realize that the marketplace is highly competitive. They also realize that because it is a buyers' market in many cases, they can insist on services that were unavailable in previous years.

Many services are developed in direct response to customer requests. The vendor may have to offer service features designed for one user with the hope that it will further differentiate the basic product as well as satisfy the immediate customer needs. The ability of the vendor to satisfy this elite market with a specialized product contributes directly to its overall success and benefits all approval plan users.

The vendor profits from this service experience in other ways. Many advanced services can be tested within the approval users group in order to determine suitability for the marketplace in general. A good example would be the use of a professional librarian sales staff. The concept of librarians as account executives was first tried in the approval plan area and found to be very successful. This organization serves as a model for the general sales force. The entire service staff benefits from the high degree of training in the specialized service areas. The special service people are more demanding of the company in general because they are serving an elite group.

These people become the role models for others involved in customer service. The vendor is able to support this high level of service because of improved purchasing terms achieved by advance quantity purchasing, fewer errors in purchasing, and a stronger position as both a buyer and seller of services. Again, libraries benefit.

Timing, comprehensiveness, and fulfillment are audited by the library. This external audit clearly shows itself in the claiming service which acts as a check not only on the approval plan but also on the vendor database in general and on related products such as standing order services.

The vendor also has the responsibility for auditing itself. It should do this through studies of fulfillment. Another vendor audit should be performed regularly on the open order files. Customer-submitted claims as well as the previously mentioned CIP and MARC records can and should be used by the vendor to monitor performance in the area of data gathering. An essential audit is that on the publisher control mechanism. Here the vendor does what many single libraries cannot afford to do, that is, monitor thousands of publishers on a regular basis throughout the year. In all areas, the vendor must be willing to ask the user, "How am I doing?"

As a provider of approval plan services, the vendor's image in the academic marketplace is very positive. The vendor's dedication to servicing this market is obvious to anyone who is aware of the vendor resources required to support an approval plan. The academic librarian realizes that the presence of an approval plan has a beneficial effect on the vendor's entire operation and that the service to all types of libraries is improved. It also is increasingly obvious that the internal requirements for an approval plan – bibliographic control, publisher contact, customer service, etc. – have become the core of the vendor's entire fulfillment operation. From this perspective, it is clear that any vendor having an approval plan has a strong commitment to the academic library. The vendor's presence in other markets – public library, retail bookstore, and school library – is built upon its services to the approval plan users and academic market, and not the other way around.

This marketplace diversification actually ensures the survival of the vendor because, during an economic downturn, each market is in a different time frame as it reacts to a long or short period of depression. The initial reaction and budget recovery for each market are unique, giving the vendor the stability required in a recession. In other words, as one market reacts to generalized budget reduction, other markets are still holding their own. As one begins a recovery, another starts to experience a decline. This cyclical nature of the various marketplaces allows the vendor to maintain the level of sales required to support all activities. Marketplace diversification is a corporate strategy designed to protect both vendor and customer.

The approval plan vendor must also be able and willing to accept a leadership role in the library industry. Its products will, naturally, be of higher quality than those of its competitors. In fact, many of its products set the standards for the industry.

Although an approval plan service benefits the vendor and its customers in many ways, significant challenges are involved in its successful operation. One of the greatest is the development of good communications between the approval plan user and the vendor. An academic vendor knows that the transition to an approval plan must be skillfully handled to ensure continuity in the development of a collection. A strong communication link is of utmost importance for the purpose of establishing a profile. The approval plan user has to convey its needs to the vendor through the profile which becomes a mirror image of collection development policies. Robert Sewell, the Western European Acquisitions Coordinator, University of Illinois Library at Urbana-Champaign, points out that "developing profiles, which guide the vendor in selection, is a way to gain control over automatic acquisitions as well as a way of involving teaching faculty in collection development."[1]

How can a strong link be developed? The vendor's representatives must be able to present the plan. A professional who has worked in a university library knows the techniques and challenges of collection development and will more effectively develop communications between the library and the vendor. Additionally, the vendor representative should be available thereafter for periodic visits and for consultation concerning all aspects of the plan. On the other hand, it is the library's responsibility to have a well-qualified person representing the library as liaison between the library and the vendor. This person should have general knowledge of collection development policies, budget requirements, and procedures for acquiring library materials. The installation of the plan is made easier, and the plan will run more smoothly if these criteria for the representatives of the vendor and of the library are met and the communications are firmly established.

Another challenge is meeting the library's expectations. All too often vendors fail to ask prospective approval plan users what they expect the plan to do for their libraries. When the library expects the approval plan to enhance the current collection development procedures and to act as an additional method of selecting books, the implementation of the plan should be smooth and easy. However, if a prospective user fears that the plan will compromise his or her selection responsibility, then the vendor has failed in the presentation of the concept. An approval plan vendor with many years of experience is aware that attitudes are very important to the effectiveness of a plan. The library's expectations can be met if the vendor's role vis-a-vis the librarian's role is clearly defined. From the vendor's perspective, the major role of the vendor is to identify and supply titles, and the librarian's role is to select from these titles.

Another challenge occurs when the library expects an approval plan to answer all or almost all its collection development needs for current imprints. Although that is one of the major goals of a vendor with a large comprehensive plan, some publishers are not willing to sell to a wholesaler. It is estimated that there are approximately five hundred such publishers who prefer to handle individual orders only. Therefore, libraries using an approval plan must be prepared to order some titles "outside" their plan.

There are also environmental factors that affect the vendor. Through the sixties and into the mid-seventies, budgets were such that increases in book prices were of minor concern to libraries running approval plans. However, in the late seventies and into the eighties, the increased cost of books and the reduction in book budgets presented a challenge for approval plan vendors. Especially toward the end of fiscal years, there is a noticeable increase in return rates or, in a few cases, the cessation of automatic shipments. Effective communication can aid in reducing book shipments until budgets are again meeting the needs of the libraries. Today, the vendor must prepare an increased number of budget estimates based on profiles and must supply more management reports than ever. Profile changes can effectively help the user to stay within budget requirements. Vendors who have efficient methods of refining profiles, preparing budget estimates, and supplying management reports can meet this environmental challenge with little difficulty.

The control of library acquisitions by the teaching faculty is another environmental factor. From the beginning, the experienced vendor knows that this factor may mean higher return rates, more frequent profile changes, and possible dissatisfaction. Return rates are usually higher because of the teaching faculty's inability to see how specific titles can be used in other subject or curriculum areas; thus titles are rejected only to be requested later. Profile changes will occur more frequently because of the turnover in teaching faculty. The interests of new faculty members may differ from those of their predecessors. Again to quote Robert Sewell, "It is the responsibility of large academic and research libraries to develop quality, and whenever possible, broadly based collections not subject to monetary whims."[2] Vendors have to meet the challenge of faculty control in the best way possible, using all of the resources available – meetings with teaching faculty to explain the approval plan concept, to detail internal procedures, and to review profiles.

Turnover in library personnel also can affect the approval plan. The presence of new personnel can mean the vendor may have to deal with someone who is opposed to the approval plan concept, someone who has never used an approval plan, or someone who has used another vendor's program and feels uncomfortable with the unfamiliar. The vendor has to meet this challenge by re-selling the concept to the new people in charge.

*Conclusion*

The academic vendor sees university and research libraries as a viable marketplace for a service that is beneficial both to the libraries and to the vendor. The impact of a successful approval plan is great. As a product, the plan requires tremendous resources from the vendor. There is, however, a synergistic effect, and all the services offered by the vendor are improved. The librarian, as a manager of the book purchasing function, is able to improve the quality of the acquisitions program by selecting an approval plan.

The future of the approval plan depends on how well vendors continue to meet the needs and the challenges involved in the successful operation of this unique and elite service. The successful vendor will keep abreast of the changing needs of the marketplace and will face with confidence the challenges brought about by this changing market. An approval plan is just plain good business for the vendor and for the library.

## Notes

1. Sewell, Robert G., "Managing European Automatic Acquisitions," *Library Resources & Technical Services* v. 27, no. 4 (October/December 1983): 403.

2. Sewell, p404.

## BIBLIOGRAPHY

by

Rodney M. Hersberger

The acquisition of materials for libraries has always been a subject generating much written and verbal comment. The literature of the profession is full of quality commentary, description, reporting and opinion about library acquisitions. This bibliography was prepared to suggest readings to supplement the theme of the conference – issues in acquisitions. By necessity the groupings in the bibliography do not exactly duplicate the titles of the preceding papers. Rather, the entries are arranged topically to offer further reading opportunities in the continuing issues in acquisitions. No entry is more than ten years old.

### APPROVAL PLANS

Berkner, D.S. "Considerations in Selecting an Approval Plan," in International Conference on Approval Plans and Collection Development (Milwaukee, 1979). *Shaping Library Collections for the 1980s*. Oryx Press, 1980. p. 143–158.

Cargill, J.S. and Alley, B. *Practical Approval Plan Management*. Oryx Press, 1979. 95p.

DeVilbiss, M.L. "Approval-Built Collection in the Medium-Sized Academic Library," *College and Research Libraries*, 36:487--492 (November 1975).

Hulbert, L.A. and Curry, D.S. "Evaluation of an Approval Plan," *College and Research Libraries*, 39:485--491 (November 1978).

International Conference on Approval Plans and Collection Development (Milwaukee, 1979). *Shaping Library Collections for the 1980s*. Oryx Press, 1980. 235p.

McCullough, K. and others. *Approval Plans and Academic Libraries:*

*An Interpretive Survey*, Oryx Press, 1977. 154p.

McDonald, D.R. and others. "Sequential Analysis: A Methodology for Monitoring Approval Plans," *College and Research Libraries*, 40:329–334 (July 1979).

Mosher, P.H. "Waiting for Godot: Rating Approval Service Vendors," in International Conference on Approval and Collection Development (Milwaukee, 1979). *Shaping Library Collections for the 1980s*. Oryx Press, 1980. p. 159--166.

Newborn, D.E. and Godden, I.P. "Improving Approval Plan Performance: A Case Study," *Library Acquisitions: Practice and Theory*, 4 (no. 2):145--155 (1980).

Perrault, A.H. "New Dimension in Approval Plan Service," *Library Acquisitions: Practice and Theory*, 7 (no. 1):35--40 (1983).

Posey, E.D. and McCullough, K. "Approval Plans One Year Later: The Purdue Experience with Separate School Plans," in American Library Association. Association of College and Research Libraries. *New Horizons for Academic Libraries*, Saur Verlag, 1979. p. 483--489.

Reidelbach, J.H. and Shirk, G.M. "Selecting an Approval Plan Vendor: A Step-by-Step Process," *Library Acquisitions: Practice and Theory*, 7 (no. 2):115--125 (1983).

Vosper, R.G. "Blanket Order: Some Historical Footnotes and Conjectures," in International Conference on Approval Plans and Collection Development (Milwaukee, 1979). *Shaping Library Collections for the 1980s*, Oryx Press, 1980. p. 4--17.

## PROCESSING ISSUES IN ACQUISITIONS

American Library Association. Resources and Technical Services Division. Resources Section. Bookdealer-Library Relations Committee. *Guide-Lines for Handling Library Orders for Microforms*, American Library Association, 1977. 14p.

"ANSI Issues New Standard for Ordering Single Titles," *Library Journal*, 107:2208 (Dec. 1, 1982).

Archer, J.D. "Preorder Searching in Academic Libraries: A Bibliographic Essay," *Library Acquisitions: Practice and Theory*, 7 (no. 2):139--144 (1983).

Baumfield, B.H. "Acquisitions Processes and Preparation for Use," in *Manual of Library Economy*, Shoe String; C. Bingley, 1977. p. 188--199.

Bloomberg, M. and Evans, G.E. "Order Procedures," in *Introduction to Technical Services for Library Technicians*, Libraries Unlimited, 1981. p. 108--120.

Bloomberg, M. and Evans, G.E. "Records and Files of the Acquisition Department," *Introduction to Technical Services for Library Technicians*, Libraries Unlimited, 1981. p. 135--140.

"Book Buyers and Book Sellers: The Business of Acquisitions," *Library Acquisitions: Practice and Theory*, 3 (no. 1): 3--17 (1979).

Bullard, S.R. "Acquisitions Preconference 3: The Comprehensive Report," *Library Acquisitions: Practice and Theory*, 4 (nos. 3–4):173--180 (1980).

Bullard, S.R. "Booksellers Discussion Group: Toward Standardized Formats for Electronic Purchase Orders," *Library Acquisitions: Practice and Theory*, 6 (no. 3):239–240 (1982).

Cenzer, P.S. "Retrospective Buying Using an Approval Plan Database," in International Conference on Approval Plans and Collection Development (Milwaukee, 1979). *Shaping Library Collections for the 1980s*, Oryx Press, 1980. p. 79--83.

Conway, S. and others. "Selection and Acquisitions Manual Development," *Medical Library Association Bulletin*, 67:54--58 (January, 1979).

Culpepper, J.C. "Recent Application of [Acquisitions] Survey Instrument: A Viable Alternative," *Kentucky Libraries*, 45:3–7 (Fall 1981).

DePew, J.N. "Acquisitions Decision Model for Academic Libraries," *American Society for Information Science Journal*, 26:237--246 (July, 1975).

Fraley, R.A. "Publishers vs. Wholesalers: The Ordering Dilemma," *Library Acquisitions: Practice and Theory*, 3 (no. 1):9--13 (1979).

Groot, E.H. "Comparison of Library Tools for Monograph Verification," *Library Resources and Technical Services*, 25:149--161 (April, 1981).

Halwas, R.G. "Buying Books from Dealers," in *Book Collecting, A Modern Guide*, Bowker, 1977. p. 26–37.

Hodowanec, G.B. "Acquisition Rate Model for Academic Libraries," *College and Research Libraries*, 39:439--447 (November 1978).

Kennedy, G. and Bullard, S.R. "Discounts and Returns, Bidding and Contracts, and Good Ol' Gifts: A Report on the ALA/RTSD Acquisition of Library Materials Discussion Group Held February 1, 1981, Washington, D.C.," *Library Acquisitions: Practice and Theory*, 5 (no. 1):39--44 (1981).

Kim, U.C. *Policies of Publishers; A Handbook for Order Librarians*, Scarecrow, 1982. 161p.

Lincoln, R. "Controlling Duplicate Orders; Or, Riding a Camel," *Library Acquisitions: Practice and Theory*, 2 (nos. 3--4):143--150 (1978).

Miller, B.C. "Placing and Tracing Orders in a Dynamic Acquisitions Process," *Collection Management*, 3:233-246 (Summer-Fall 1979).

Neikirk, H.D. "Less Does More: Adapting Pre-Order Searching to On-Line Cataloging," *Library Acquisitions: Practice and Theory*, 5, no. 2:89--94 (1981).

Paul, S.K. "New Era in Order Fulfillment?" *Publishers Weekly*, 213: 36--37 (April 10, 1978).

Schenck, W.Z. "Claiming [Monographs]: Luxury or Necessity?" *Library Acquisitions: Practice and Theory*, 5 (no. 1):3--7 (1981).

Stewart, C.C. "Update on Ordering Standards," *Information Technology and Libraries*, 1:341--343 (December 1983).

Wynar, B.S. "Ordering Books for Academic Libraries: Some Myths and Realities," in Louisiana. State University, Baton Rouge. Graduate School of Library Science. *Library Lectures, Numbers Twenty-One through Twenty-Eight*, Louisiana State University Library, 1975. p. 25--31.

Ashley, P. "NOTIS [Northwestern On-Line Total Integrated System] in Action: Acquiring Materials with an Integrated System," *Illinois Libraries* 64:56--67 (January 1982).

Association of Research Libraries. Systems and Procedures Exchange Center. *Approval Plans in ARL Libraries*, The Center, 1982. 109p.

"Automated Acquisitions and the Shared Database: A Meeting of the RTSD Discussion Group on Automated Acquisitions/In-Process Control Systems," *Library Acquisitions: Practice and Theory*, 7 (no. 2):89--107 (1983).

"Automated Acquisitions Systems; Papers Presented at the LITA Institute," *Journal of Library Automation*, 13:155--195 (September 1980) and 13:221--264 (December 1980).

Bonk, S.C. "Integrating Library and Book Trade Automation," *Information Technology and Libraries*, 2:18--25 (March 1983).

Boss, R.W. and Marcum, D.H. "On-Line Acquisitions Systems for Libraries," *Library Technology Reports*, March/April 1981.

Bruer, J.M. "Management Information Aspects of Automated Acquisitions Systems," *Library Resources & Technical Services*, 24: 339--342 (Fall 1980).

Bullard, S.R. "OLAS: One Library's Experience," *Library Acquisitions: Practice and Theory*, 5 (no. 2):73–80 (1981).

Calhoun, J.C. and Bracken, J.K. "Automated Acquisitions and Collection Development in the Knox College Library," *Information Technology and Libraries*, 1:246–256 (September 1982).

Cargill, J.S. "On-Line Acquisitions: Use of a Vendor System," *Library Acquisitions: Practice and Theory*, 4 (nos. 3--4):236--245 (1980).

Cargill, J.S. and Alley, B. "Use of a Commercial Acquisitions System," *Ohio Library Association Bulletin*, 50:26--27 (July 1980).

Davis, M.B. "Model for a Vendor Study in a Manual or Semi-Automated Acquisitions System," *Library Acquisitions: Practice and Theory*, 3 (no. 1):53--60 (1979).

Doebler, P.D. "Computer-to-Computer Communication Is Picking Up Steam," *Publishers Weekly*, 216:370--371 (August 27, 1979).

Doebler, P.D. "New Standard Data Format Hastens Computer Ordering," *Publishers Weekly*, 212:88 (December 12, 1977).

Franz, T. "Automated Standing Order System, Blackwell North America," *Serials Review*, 7:63–67 (January 1981).

Furlong, E.J. "Case Study in Automated Acquisitions: Northwestern University Library," *Journal of Library Automation*, 13:222--240 (December 1980).

Griffin, D.E. and Ziegman, B. "Automated Serials Acquisitions in the Washington Library Network," in *Management of Serials Automation*, Haworth Press, 1982. p. 237--243.

Heyman, B.L. and Abbott, G.L., comps. "Automated Acquisitions: A Bibliography," *Library Technology Reports*, 17:195--202 (March/April 1981).

Hines, T.C. and others. "Library Applications of Microcomputers," *Wyoming Library Roundup*, 37:33--40 (Spring 1982).

Hogan, W.P. "Acquisitions Roundtable: Limitations of the OCLC Search as a Means of PreOrder Duplicate Detection," *Library Acquisitions: Practice and Theory*, 7 (no. 1):21--22 (1983).

Hogan, W.P. "Ringgold's Nonesuch Acquisitions System: One Year After Installation," *Library Acquisitions: Practice and Theory*, 6 (no. 1):41--45 (1982).

"IROS [Instant Response Ordering System] at the University of Southern California," *Journal of Academic Librarianship*, 3: 220--221 (September 1977).

Leightty, V.L. and Nixon, N.D. "Interfacing OCLC and DataPhase for an Automated Acquisitions System," *Library Acquisitions: Practice and Theory*, 6 (no. 3):259--263 (1982).

Leonhardt, T.W. "Duke University Library Automated Acquisitions System," *Library Acquisitions: Practice and Theory*, 5 (nos. 3--4):185--191 (1981).

Leung, S.W. "INNOVACQ 100 System: Experience of a Pilot User,"

*Library Acquisitions: Practice and Theory*, 7 (no. 2):127--138 (1983).

Long, J.K. "Electronic Order Transmission," *Journal of Library Automation*, 14:295--297 (December 1981).

Lukac, J. "Evolution of an Online Acquisitions System," *Journal of Library Automation*, 14:100--101 (June 1981).

Malinconico, S.M. "Planning for Failure [Introducing Automation]," *Library Journal*, 108:798--800 (April 15, 1983).

Matthews, J.R. "Automated Library System Marketplace, 1982: Change and More Change!" *Library Journal*, 108:547--553 (March 15, 1983).

Neikirk, H.D. "Automated Acquisitions Discussions Group," *Library Acquisitions: Practice and Theory*, 6 (no. 3):247--249 (1982).

Paul, S.K. "Computer-to-Computer Communication in the Acquisition Process," *Journal of Library Automation*, 14:299--303 (December 1981).

Popovich, M. and Miller, B. "Online Ordering with Dialorder," *Online*, 5:63--65 (April 1981).

Potter, W.G. "Automated Acquisitions in Academic Libraries," *Illinois Libraries*, 62:637--639 (September 1980).

Potter, W.G. "LCS for Acquisitions [at the University of Illinois]," *Illinois Libraries* 64:68--70 (January 1982).

"WLN Begins Electronic Book Ordering," *Wilson Library Bulletin*, 57:377 (January 1983).

Ziegman, B. and Aveney, B.H. "WLN Online Order Transmission," *Information Technology and Libraries*, 1:346--348 (December 1982).

## VENDOR PRACTICES AND PERFORMANCE

Anthony, D.J. "Customer Service: Order Fulfillment as Communication," *Scholarly Publishing*, 7:343--352 (July 1976).

Duchin, D. and Secor, J.R. "Manual Continuations Processing at

Yankee Book Peddler, Inc.," *Serials Review*, 6:79--84 (July 1980).

Grant, J. and Perelmuter, S. "Vendor Performance Evaluation," *Journal of Academic Librarianship*, 4:366--367 (November 1978).

Lincoln, R. "Vendors and Delivery, an Analysis of Selected Publishers, Publisher/Agents, Distributors, and Wholesalers," *Canadian Library Journal*, 35:51--5+ (February 1978).

Lindsey, J.A. "Vendor Discounts to Libraries in a Consortium," *Library Acquisitions: Practice and Theory*, 5 (nos. 3--5):147--152 (1981).

Maddox, W.J. "Serials Management at Otto Harrassowitz," *Serials Review*, 7:75--77 (July 1981).

Stephens, D. "Library Materials and Their Acquisition: The Vendor Point of View," *Sourdough*, 17:14 (May/June 1980).

Stokley, S.L. and Reid, M.T. "Study of Performance of Five Book Dealers Used by Louisiana State University Library," *Library Resources and Technical Services*, 22:117--125 (Spring 1978).

## FINANCIAL AND ACCOUNTING ASPECTS IN ACQUISITIONS

American Library Association. Resources and Technical Services Division. Resources Section. Bookdealer--Library Relations Committee. "Prepayment Dilemma: A Consumer's Guide," *American Libraries*, 8:571--572 (November 1977).

Evans, G.T. "Cost of Information about Library Acquisition Budgets," *Collection Management*, 2:3–23 (Spring 1978).

Leider, R. "How Librarians Help Inflate the Price of Books, and What to Do about It: A Publisher's View," *American Libraries*, 11:559--560 (October 1980).

Lynden, F.C. "Library Materials Budgeting in the Private University Library: Austerity and Action," in *Advances in Librarianship*, vol. 10, Academic Press, 1980. p. 89--154.

Maher, W.J. "Measurement and Analysis of Processing Costs in Academic Archives," *College and Research Libraries*, 43:59--67

(January 1982).

Kohut, J.J. "Allocating the Book Budget: A Model," *College and Research Libraries*, 35:192–199 (May 1974).

McPheron, W.G. "Quantifying the Allocation of Monograph Funds: An Instance in Practice," *College and Research Libraries*, 44: 116--127 (March 1983).

Pierce, T.J. "Empirical Approach to the Allocation of the University Library Book Budget," *Collection Management*, 2:38--58 (Spring 1978).

Reid, M.T. "Coping with Budget Adversity: The Impact of the Financial Squeeze on Acquisitions," *College and Research Libraries*, 37:266--272 (May 1976).

Reid, M.T. "Pitfalls of Prepayments," *Louisiana Library Association Bulletin*, 40:66--67 (Winter 1978).

Sampson, G.S. "Allocating the Book Budget: Measuring for Inflation," *College and Research Libraries*, 39:381–383 (September 1978).

Sauer, T. "Predicting Book Fund Expenditures: A Statistical Model," *College and Research Libraries*, 39:474--478 (November 1978).

Snowball, G.J. and Cohen, M.S. "Control of Book Fund Expenditures under an Accrual Accounting System," *Collection Management*, 3:5--20 (Spring 1979).

Speller, B.F. "Purchasing for Libraries and Information Centers: Part IIA – Bids and Contracts," *Library Acquisitions: Practice and Theory*, 5 (no. 1): 31--37 (1981).

Sweetman, P. and Wiedemann, P. "Developing a Library Book-Fund Allocation Formula," *Journal of Academic Librarianship*, 6:268--276 (November 1980).

Uden, J. "Financial Reporting and Vendor Performance: A Case Study," *Journal of Library Automation*, 13:185--195 (September 1980).

Wright, C.D. and Watkins, J.F. "Allocating the Higher Education Book Budget; A Process That Works," *Educational Technology*, 17:58--60 (March 1977).

# Index

Richard Abel Company 59, 91, 92
Adams, Scott 98
American Library Association (ALA) 6, 7
American Library Association. Bookdealer Relations Committee 6, 8, 9
American Library Association. Library Education Division 6
American Library Association. Resources and Technical Services Division 6
American Library Association. Resources and Technical Services Division. Collection Management and Development Committee 1, 6, 11
approval plan(s) 7, 11, 12, 13, 14, 15, 16, 18, 19, 20, 22, 23, 25, 27, 33, 34, 35, 36, 37, 39, 40, 41, 42, 47, 48, 49, 50, 51, 56, 57, 58, 59, 60, 86, 91, 92, 93, 94, 95, 96, 97, 98, 100, 101, 102, 103, 104, 105, 106, 111, 112, 113, 114, 115, 116, 117, 118, 119
Argyres, Claudia 15, 16
Association of Research Libraries (ARL) 59
automation 6, 69, 70, 71, 72, 73, 92, 101, 105
Axford, H. William 103
Baker & Taylor 59, 60, 95, 105
Ballen 95
Bertram Rota 59
Biblarz, Dora 13, 23, 25
B. H. Blackwell 94, 95
Blackwell North America 93, 94, 95, 103, 104
Boise State University 34
book(s) 2, 3, 4, 11, 12, 14, 16, 22, 24, 26, 41, 42, 46, 48, 50, 56, 57, 58, 60, 61, 62, 63, 64, 91, 92, 93, 94, 95, 98, 99, 102, 105, 111, 112, 113, 114, 115, 117, 118, 119
Boyer, Calvin 104
budget(s) 2, 20, 23, 82, 92, 94, 102, 117, 118
Busse, David 96

California State University – Long Beach 106
Cargill, Jennifer 15
Cenzer, Pamela S. 104
Churchman, C. West 18
collection development 33, 34, 35, 36, 48, 49, 51, 55, 56, 57, 58, 59, 60, 62, 92, 96, 102, 103, 104, 111, 115, 117
college(s) 55, 56
communication(s) 8, 14, 15, 19, 25, 26, 34, 72, 75, 96, 100, 117
conference proceedings 35, 45, 46, 48, 49

cost(s) 2, 6, 12, 14, 16, 17, 28, 51, 70, 71, 73, 74, 76, 84, 86, 91, 94, 98, 99, 101, 102, 112, 113, 118
credit 22, 62, 63
Curry, David 11

dealer(s) 2, 3, 7, 8, 11, 12, 13
discount(s) 3, 4, 5, 17, 22, 24, 58, 98, 105, 112, 115

Early, Caroline 1
Elsevier 46
Evans, G. Edward 2, 15, 16

faculty 13, 16, 35, 36, 41, 42, 46, 55, 56, 57, 58, 60, 61, 62, 63, 64, 97, 99, 101, 117, 118
feedback 5, 19, 25, 26, 28, 57
Fraser, Wendy 11, 15

Gates, Christopher 5
George Washington University 1, 106
Godden, Irene 105
Gregor, Jan 11, 15

Otto Harrassowitz 59
Heitshu, Sara 1
Henderson, Gay 1
Hensel, Evelyn 6
Howard University 105
humanities 45
Hulbert, Linda 11

Indiana State University 3
interlibrary loan 42, 46

jobber 2, 34, 106
journal 42, 49, 104

Landesman, Margaret 5
Leonhart, Thomas 1, 11, 34
librarian(s) 2, 4, 6, 7, 8, 9, 15, 16, 33, 35, 36, 37, 48, 49, 50, 51, 55, 56, 58, 59, 60, 62, 63, 72, 87, 96, 97, 98, 100, 101, 105, 106, 114, 115, 118, 119
Library of Congress 1
LIBRIS 96
Louisiana State University 1, 2

McCullough, Kathleen 29
management 4, 6, 7, 55, 70, 72, 85, 113, 115, 118
measure 19, 24, 25, 27, 28
measurement 18, 20, 26, 27
Melcher, Daniel 5, 7, 25
monograph(s) 6, 7, 35, 37, 39, 42, 112
Mosher, Paul 13
Nader, Ralph 3
National League of Cities 6
Newborn, Dennis 105

OCLC 40, 42, 104
Ohio State University 1

performance 1, 2, 4, 7, 8, 11, 12, 13, 14, 15, 16, 17, 18, 19, 20, 22, 23, 24, 25, 26, 27, 28, 33, 34, 63, 75, 85, 87
Plenum 46
Pletzke, Linda 1
profile 13, 14, 24, 27, 36, 41, 42, 49, 56, 57, 60, 63, 97, 99, 100, 101, 102, 106, 115, 117

publisher(s) 4, 5, 6, 12, 17, 20, 22, 35, 36, 39, 41, 42, 45, 46, 48, 51, 91, 92, 93, 94, 98, 99, 100, 102, 104, 105, 111, 112, 116, 118
publishing 26, 96, 98

Reid, Marion 1, 2, 3
Reidelbach, John 20
research 34, 37, 42, 46, 57
return rate 17, 63, 100, 113

science 34, 37, 41, 45, 46
selection(s) 15, 16, 20, 22, 23, 24, 34, 36, 46, 48, 50, 55, 58, 59, 62, 63, 64, 69, 78, 89, 94, 95, 99, 102, 106
selectors 77, 80
serial(s) 6, 61, 83, 86, 98
service(s) 2, 3, 4, 5, 7, 8, 12, 13, 14, 16, 20, 22, 23, 24, 59, 60, 95, 99, 100, 111, 112, 113, 115, 116, 119
Sewell, Robert 117, 118
Shirk, Gary 20
Smith, F. Seymour 99
social science 45
Springer-Verlag 46
Stokley, Sandra 2, 3

Texas A&M University 34, 35, 37, 45, 47
Trinity University 105

Uden, Janet 8
university 3, 37, 45, 55, 56, 59, 111, 117, 119
University of Florida 104
University of Illinois 117
University of Massachusetts 8
University of Michigan 1, 70, 71
University of Mississippi 104
University of Missouri 70, 71
University of Oregon 1
University of Utah 5
university press(es) 34, 45, 46, 47, 48, 51, 99, 103

Veillette, Peter 6

Washington University 59, 64
Wiley 46
Wolf, Milton 12